C000216343

Fishing
Personally

W. M. HILL

A & C Black · London

Published by A & C Black (Publishers) Ltd.
35 Bedford Row, London, WC1R 4JH

© W. M. Hill 1986

First published 1986

All rights reserved. No part of this publication may be
reproduced, stored in a retrieval system, or transmitted,
in any form or by any means, electronic, mechanical,
photocopying or otherwise, without the prior permission
of the publishers.

Hill, W.M.
  Fishing personally.
  1. Salmon-fishing—Great Britain
  2. Trout-fishing—Great Britain
  I.Title
  799.1'2   SA684

  ISBN 0-7136-5573-9

Printed in Great Britain by
Billing & Sons Limited, Worcester

Acknowledgements

The line illustrations in this book were drawn by Tony Whieldon.
The cover design was by Chris McLeod.

Contents

1   *Punk in a muddle*   1

2   *Back to brotherly balance*   7

3   *Playing to the gallery*   13

4   *On special service*   20

5   *The bronze age of leisure*   24

6   *Mighty weapons for real men*   29

7   *Doomwatching the generation gap*   34

8   *A spell on virgin water*   39

9   *Dressing the part*   46

10   *Leaves on a hot pond*   51

11   *Seasonable selfishness*   58

12   *Right against the evidence*   62

13   *Snoring in Sabland*   68

14   *A bid for Bumblies*   74

15   *Painful problem*   78

16   *What to grab when you run*   83

17   *Wonder what's in there?*   90

18   *Pub crawl*   96

19   *Indulgence (1) . . . real sin*   102

20   *Indulgence (2) . . . on the rack*   107

21   *Indulgence (3) . . . trapped!*   112

22   *Freezer fodder*   116

23   *Sunburned sportfishers*   120

24   *Don't take it so heavy, dearie*   126

25   *Shopping for porky barbel*   133

26   *Some people never learn*   138

27   *Evening class*   143

28   *Stop it right now!*   148

For today's anglers
and yesterday's angling

It must never be forgotten that each age looks at questions from its own angle and requires them to be formulated in its own terms . . . every epoch requires to say its own say.

We, too, shall grow out of date. Fishers of a hundred years hence will cast an easy smile on ourselves and our methods which we think so delicate and so final. Our tackle and our dress, our practice and our appearance, will seem to belong to the dark ages.

John Waller Hills, *A Summer on the Test* (1924)

CHAPTER ONE

Punk in a muddle

It was a fun party for information-gatherers and friendly folk in charge of the reservoir. If you were on their guest list you were invited to fish the water the day before the season opened to all those thousands who had been practising their double-haul techniques. So for one day you got first bash and did not have to stand with your elbows tucked in and all the anglers in Britain on each side of you, with their families sitting behind within range of the backcast.

Looking out from the fishing lodge, the view of the reservoir put one in mind of the one that faces men who work on drilling platforms in the North Sea. Wind and rain; waves and spume flying up the slope of the dam. Typical reservoir; typical new stillwater season; typical spring.

These guest days begin with tobacco and coffee as you pull on foul-weather gear. You study your hosts' fishing-book entries from the previous season and hear much introverted fishing talk coming from notable and significant catchers of trout. No question about it, this is a pleasant way to start the reservoir season – even if the Great Name doesn't turn up and the lesser names yarn about great things.

But there's no hardship in hovering, just for a time, on the fringe of angling Press circles. They will disappear soon enough after opening day . . . like a rise on the Itchen when your weight-forward line pounds the water and double-taper men tell you to go and pound a blasted reservoir, where it won't show so much.

We left the lodge eventually and leaned in to the wind. We made jokes and sucked pipes which were being hosed down; and we fished.

Most of the known names fished rather better than I did. On a reservoir this is usually a matter of technique, and that applies anywhere, really; or it's a matter of discovering quite quickly that the latest batch of stock fish, put in the week before, are not going by the book. When you're flogging the deeps on a cold, black day with a big, black lure, it's a bright fellow who knows that the stock has decided to sport in the shallow end.

So the rest of us moved to the shallow end on the windward bank and let rip. There was a splash to the right and a splash to the left. The one on the right was a rainbow greeting dark clouds, the one on the left was somebody who had dropped his rod in the water. He was tugging at a pile of tall brambles clutching his Baby Doll. He wasn't a *known* name.

I helped him like a Christian, and he asked for some advice. That sort of thing always makes you feel like one of the circle, which is not a good feeling. At least, it's not a good feeling when you've been wrenching at yards of wet Dacron and feeling totally out of control of the shooting head. Even with the wind's help I'd reached out over only a few yards of water and would have been better off with the weight-forward 6F with which I had lashed other small lakes and rivers that deserved better of me.

However, the man did need help. He had another Baby Doll but no knowledge of how to connect it up. He said someone at the office had lent him the rod, and he was really their motoring correspondent.

Six feet of 3 lb breaking strain treble reef-knotted to his line was a problem that could only be solved by scissors, so we snipped away and talked about needle knots, water knots, blood knots and cast-connectors – crouching by the bramble bush with the grey water waiting and the rain beating down on cold hands.

By the time they were pouring gin or the chilled Italian dry white for lunch back at the lodge, my left-hand man's Baby Doll had accounted for two fish; I'd had one; others had rather more. In fact, I reckon my score would have been better if I hadn't talked so much.

Answering the lunch call, everyone squelched back to put their rods in the racks and their plastic bags by the steps. The fish in those bags were curved and fixed in mounds of fading pink, the flesh congealing under the plastic, which stuck to their blank eyes.

Many anglers care about the presentation of the fly, but not of the trout. Had it been topical-tips day for all, I'd have told them about newspaper. A quality broadsheet is the best wrapping for trout – back home, the paper peels away, leaving the fish still looking like a creature which can command respect.

But with every hour that passes, on stillwater fisheries, craftsmen with the rod are bearing away lumps of distorted protein, and who was I, with my single fish, to deliver this splendid newsprint knowledge? Even a Great Name would know enough to keep it to himself.

In the afternoon the rain stopped and the wind increased its efforts as a consequence. We grasped our glass or carbon rods (or both) and took our fish-catchers' positions on the windward bank again. However, I felt that I would do better by communing with the trout alone, telling them that I didn't have a plastic bag, but a copy of the *Daily Telegraph*.

Being entirely alone meant the leeward bank, where nobody else wanted to go. They knew all about the problems of wind partly in the right ear and wholly against the casting arm. But this matter of space is important and

I'm blessed if I can understand how you can enjoy the day if your fly (or your float, come to that) is in some other bloke's territory and you have to peer round your bucking rod when a fish runs and say "Sorry", while the angler next door waits for you to get it over with.

Sometimes I think we should train fish as well as fishermen. No well-bred trout should run too far unless it is straight into the middle of the reservoir. Still, since this day was uncrowded anyway there was really no need to seek a whole bank for the sake of privacy. It must have been an old habit that sent me walking over the dam to that ghastly shoreline to stand in the rolling breakers while the eyes watered in the gusts out of the west.

These days it is not a matter of big trout being provided only for big people, because everybody has a chance of getting at heavyweights. We put a lot of good fish into the holes we dig. The trout farms are churning them out. In doing that, the suppliers are often colouring our rivers with effluent and probably causing trouble, but it is taking the biologists a long time to prove it.

No, it's not the fish but space which is at a premium. What you don't have – at least, not often – is a broad reservoir before you and only a black speck or two at the other end to share the day. So that's probably why I made the long walk over the dam.

I tied on a large and evil-looking Muddler Minnow and thought how pleasant it was that nobody would notice my bungling as soon as I tried to extend line in that wind. All the space you could want to flail through, everybody else small black specks. One day we shall queue for that kind of privilege and approach it through turnstiles with a micro-computer ticking off the numbers and comparing them with the known stock of fish and yardage (or "metrage") of bank. It will take only the click of a time-counter before you see the red light which locks the gate and tells you to get up earlier tomorrow because the leisure complex is full today.

There's a further refinement to this vision of the near future and it has already been described, I think, by Richard Walker. In a short piece for a magazine, he wrote of programmable mechanical fish as the likely quarry for our grandchildren in the age of pollution and over-population. Richard Walker is, of course, a Great Name. Everybody in fishing circles knows him, and his retirement from writing and controversy (1984) was a sad event. But his death on a black Friday in August 1985 left an ache in the soul. It was as if a sudden blank silence had fallen over river and lake.

It must have been in the 1960s that he wrote about angling for those artificial fish and, Lord save us, many people waving rods now believe that the sixties were the halcyon days and almost as far back as Napoleon or Hitler or King George. Nevertheless, the fish *are* still flesh (if high-protein-pellet pink) and blood (still red), though programmed by scientific feeding routines on the most cost-effective pattern in the farming process.

Muttering into the gale, I whirled my Muddler at the waves, using hope and muscle power. It smashed into one long comber and came lashing back as the wind gripped the line, giving it no chance to sink. Try again. Backcast and left-hand yank. Rod angled to undercut the wind. But the wind was everywhere and you can't undercut that – not even if you are a Great Name.

There was a kind of thump in my face and the vision in my right eye went out. The Muddler Minnow had sunk in, and when that happens you stand very still and wonder about never being able to cast straight again.

The panic lasted until I realised that the hook wasn't actually in the eye but just underneath the lower lid. The fuzzy body of the Muddler had rapped the eyeball, but the

steel was buried in skin, not cornea. A gentle pull showed
that it was in over the barb. Cutting off the nylon leader,
I reeled-up and went off, in a sort of stiff-necked shuffle,
back over the dam. The shuffle turned into a slink as I went
through the late lunch drinkers in the direction of the fishing
lodge lavatory.

Mirror, mirror on the wall, who is the idiot of us all?
Who is the chap who tells tyros about needle knots and
helps them out of bramble bushes? The blood ran rather
obviously, and I can tell anyone who hasn't tried it that
a man who walks into a fishing lodge with a size 8 Muddler
Minnow dangling under his eye doesn't get sympathy. This
is due to the courtesy of notable anglers, who pretend not
to notice, not to callousness. But perhaps they thought I
was a punk rocker.

Theoretically, what you should do when this accident
happens is snip off the barb with pliers but pliers don't seem
to be around too often. There are other methods, but I've
never got round to learning about them. In any case, with
the skin stretching rather a long way from that part of my
face, no kind of pressure could be brought on the barb.

A kind man came in, as I was tugging, and spent five
minutes trying to persuade me to go to the hospital. Then
he sighed, looked grave, and took out a large knife – the
sort, it is said, which the Swedes issue to their army. (Or
is it the Swiss? At any rate, it doesn't look like a delicate
scalpel.) He sawed at the flesh once or twice and the
Minnow swam away.

As long as there are people like *him* around I don't
mind sharing a fishing day.

CHAPTER TWO

Back to brotherly balance

Just about now, some people are beginning to notice Izaak
Walton. Others are starting to rediscover Rudyard Kipling
too, despite the fact that some of us have been saying for
years that he was nothing to be ashamed of.

If you can keep your head when all around you are
digging up the past and blaming it on the boring old here
and now, then there's nothing to worry about. It's a game
we all play – like the way I collect cane rods when everyone
else has been buying boron from astronauts.

My copy of *The Compleat Angler* was given to me by
a BBC producer who kept it in his office bookcase to
preserve his sense of balance, not to mention his sanity.
He handed it on when he retired, presumably because he
felt that its duty was done or, perhaps, that it could do the
same for me.

But aside from BBC producers with souls and
sensitivity and splendid actors of the old school, like Michael
Hordern – who has been doing an Izaak Walton one-man
show – not many of us regard the old boy as a brother.

On the muddy bank, among the bronze maggots and
flying boron, no sensible man has ever been known to
mention Walton. Old Izaak and old Charlie Cotton?
Brothers of the angle? Yerrwha?

On the chalk stream among the flashing carbon wands,
nobody's read him either, but one or two (those who cling

to Palakona) might have been to hear Mr Hordern. Possibly that is just enough to make someone bring Izaak out in paperback, with a scene from the last fishing programme on the television for the cover picture. If this happens then it might just lead the way back to forgotten fishing.

It seems to me that Izaak deserves credit mostly for writing the right book at the right time. In other words, as with most 'Classics', timing is all. If you get in first and do a good job according to the standards of the day, then you are entitled to be called the Father of Angling.

You nod to Izaak and other oldies; you don't bow to them. It is better to say "Yerrwha?" and pick your nose after landing a 14 lb barbel, than to overdo the respect due to something written over 330 years ago. Unless, of course, the solution to problems then might work for problems now.

The value in this Waltonian revival may come because we do greet fine fish with a grunt, rather than lines of poetry. Perhaps a few brothers are beginning to realise that we've pushed things too far, have become too skilful, are armed with too much weaponry. So we are searching for a new sensation by snatching greedily at the calmness of a past age. Is it the power of nostalgia? Too true it is, mate, and no messing. We grab at old Izaak because we think we may have missed something on the way to a full keepnet. And quite right too, because we have.

Everybody knows that Arcady is a future vision rather than an ancient myth and that neither is attainable, and never has been. Yet it is reasonable to use Izaak as a kind of totem figure and to measure the quality of pleasure now by what it might become with the help of rosy retrospect.

I wish I could remember who it was (it might have been old Juliana, or Izaak, or even Wayne Bloggs ghosting for a big name) who wrote that you shouldn't pursue angling pleasure too far, or use it to make money. For those who know that it is indeed the giddiest of pleasures, the most pernicious drug, that is harsh advice. The fact that it is old advice, and applies to things other than angling as well, is neither here nor there – because it is advice which is always ignored.

There was a chap in one of my fishing clubs (I belong to too many, and never take advice about pleasure) who only cared to string two aesthetic thoughts together after four pints of beer, and then only when nobody else was listening. But he fished like a genius and I envied him greatly.

He made a big decision. The issue was clear. He had to give up his wife or his fishing and the answer was . . . no contest. On the departure of the wife who, presumably, was not aware of the pleasures of angling past, ignored those in the present and wasn't going to stick around for the future, this man continued merrily along.

The point to grasp, though, is that it wasn't a case of the Sunday fishing widow – which is a boring cliché scarely worth the thought – but the Monday and Wednesday one as well. It is now some time since I have seen his name in the match winners' lists so he may have hung up his rods after all and joined Anglers Anonymous. If he has, then let's all give him some moral support.

We could, with confidence, send him the paperback version of Izaak's book, because it would offer two beneficial effects. Either it would send him to sleep (since he'll learn nothing about shotting patterns and things) or it will make him think about fishing being more than just catching fish. Incidentally, *that* bit of wisdom came later than Walton. Writers of the twenties, thirties and forties knew it was more than just catching fish. However, that rarely stopped them from writing about the creel strap biting into the shoulder under such a satisfactory weight of trout, and so on.

I had a friend who took to fishing late in life and found it was all that he had been missing. He begrudged the minutes spent tying on a fly because it held him from the action. Yet he would never fish more than one day a week. Even after he retired he set aside one day only and looked forward to it with the deepest impatience. He gave up when he could no longer see the fly on the water and thought back not at all. He was a man with an essential calmness.

An angler like that is unlikely to find himself in the famous fisherman's hell, doomed to take another, and bigger, trout from the spot at which he took the last and will take the next and the next until he pleads to be allowed to miss one.

Some men have found that a dose of Izaak can slow down the frantic rush towards obsession. Those who have shuddered at themselves for calling two chub a bad day when they expected ten, should take a pause and have a shudder.

Perhaps the saving grace comes with age and the discovery that you aren't such a good angler after all, or any more. Looking over the shoulders of young lions (that is, people who think that I might have known Izaak Walton personally) you see co-ordination of hand, eye and instinct running side by side with extraordinary energy.

You find yourself wondering if all these qualities might not be better used at Olympics-level épée. The grin of satisfaction at their catch-rate has the same dashing, athletic look about it as is represented by their insignia. Arms, loaded with badges advertising tackle-manufacturers names, rise, fall, probe, tense, and act precisely at all times.

Some of us old men have been heard to grumble at club competitions which are now almost always only five hours long (sometimes three) whereas once you fished the whole day through. But even in the age of carbon, five hours of concentrated catching is enough until NFA rules are altered so as to allow substitutes to come onto the battleground.

The trouble is that bemedalled lions and badge-bearers too often show irritation if they don't catch enough fish to satisfy either their own standards, or the demands of the team captain. If they keep fishing diaries then they must be about norms rather than the sheen on a grayling's flank which so quickly fades.

Now I know why one of the best anglers around here at the moment told me, in a rare philosophical mood, that he thought he'd be finished at thirty because his reflexes wouldn't be good enough. Actually, he's past thirty now and still seems to be doing well, but perhaps he's just pacing himself properly.

For those who (like me) see a bit of themselves in all this, here are the signs to watch out for: are you irritated by people who wander up and down the bank, trying a swim here, another there, and using unsuitable tackle for each of them while appearing to enjoy it? Are you too busy studying exploded engineering drawings of the works of a new fixed-spool reel to read Izaak Walton? Do you keep a fishing diary, not for the pleasure of recapturing happy days, but as a measure of your progress towards stardom? And here's the really nasty one – do you start fidgeting after half an hour without a bite and begin to wonder if you really *are* enjoying it after all and mightn't you do better with the épée?

If you scored high in this simple test then take up the épée (provided you are under thirty, of course) thus making space on the river bank for someone else. On the other hand, if you want a cure, and Izaak hasn't got it, then go fishing with someone like John Piper, who came as my guest on a stretch of the Hampshire Avon for his last Sunday in Britain. He was packing his furniture and his memories for a new life in Spain, and taking only one rod with him. This was after years spent in the communications business, many of them as a notable angling columnist.

John fished on that spring day with a kind of natural charm and a quiet happiness which had been his approach to the world of water when we first met twenty years before. I caught nothing. He caught nothing, though, for an instant, he had seen the flash of a turning fish coming short to his spinner just below the weir.

At the end of that quiet, fishless day he thanked me. He was really thanking the river for the privilege of being beside it in spring.

Walton would have understood.

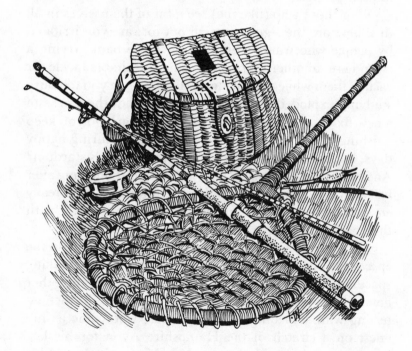

CHAPTER THREE

Playing to the gallery

Talking of angling books – which is what I'll be doing again later on – those about salmon are the ones to watch, especially if you are feeling sore or unfulfilled in that direction.

A recent one, which I read, was packed with good advice and completely spoiled by the grandest and most fatuous apology ever seen in print. The author began his book by saying that he knew his record wasn't as good as some others in the past. He was very sorry that he had caught only 1,300 salmon. Well, to the devil with that for a game of credentials! We can only hope that all the people who bought his book weren't teetering on the edge of inferiority complexes. Actually, the book deserved to do well, despite its painful opening, and perhaps salmon fishers as a breed expect that kind of thing anyway. For the rest of us, though, a score of 1,300 isn't angling, it's dreaming. Or it's magic.

Some might think that it's not a good idea to keep a tally of fish caught. On this day or that it may be reasonable to say "Had a few", "Had a brace", or "Had a netful" – depending on whether you are trouting or roaching. But we all realise (or do we?) that seeking salmon means having to be content with a large number of blank days, which is probably why talking about the occasional success is not only understandable but a necessity. How else could you keep going?

The point about any kind of angling is that it makes you think – and if it doesn't, then you aren't an angler: you're an idler on the end of a fishing rod. My view, for what it's worth, is that coarse fishing makes you think hardest, then trout fishing so close behind as hardly to matter. Salmon fishing is not for thinkers and worriers, or even for scratchers after that extra small thing which will turn the next snagged boulder into a 35-pounder. Salmon fishing is one part being in the right place at the right time and three parts luck.

Of course, all that proves is that I would catch more salmon if I'd only take the prejudice out of my typewriter and learn how to avoid being a bungler, or be less lazy, or just do something about raising more money to spend on famous rivers.

Perhaps we all need to sit at the feet of the man who has caught only 1,300 salmon. Then we'd talk about epic days and great triumphs, and everybody would listen and say "That chap knows his stuff", and be respectful and invite us to fish their famous rivers.

All I can say is that I've ground out a few days here and there with the Toby and the Devon. Not with the fly though. Once I planned a long visit to Scotland and part of the preparation was wondering about buying a fly rod. After walking around the racks in the tackle shop, gnawing my pipe and pondering, I bought three Wye leads instead, and went away.

I think it was the size of the things that put me off – that, and lack of confidence. A salmon fly rod is a pole. More of a pole when cane was king, probably less of a pole now, since I suppose they make them in carbon fibre these days. I said "lack of confidence" only to whip in a bit of honesty which I might have missed the first time round.

That moment in the tackle shop was largely to do with experience, I think. Hardly anybody fly fishes my home river, but it always seems to me that if you are hoping to irritate a fish into opening its mouth, then a Devon's bigger and more irritating than a fly.

Experience also takes you a bit further. It shows that if you are geared up for a whole season's-worth of fishless days then a set of spinning tackle is an investment quite heavy enough for that, without adding a fly kit to the account. And imagine feeling that you just *had* to go on and buy some chest waders as well; and a wading staff. Long ago, therefore, I left Jock Scott and Silver Doctor to be pickled in aspic or set in plastic brooches for tourists. And anybody who thinks this shows that I've never caught a salmon can easily force me into revealing that my score is not much more than half a dozen fish.

Now I want to talk about the last of those fish, taken only a short while ago. Others came from different times and places – mostly on Devons and one on cheese (which is a story in itself – but as cheese probably doesn't count, I won't tell it).

The latest salmon then. This fish pleased me because it came to a home-made Devon. After so much disenchantment, after so much contact with that massive luck element in salmon fishing, and after the discovery of that most unlikely feeling of boredom I began to begrudge the cost of shop Devons.

So, in order to inject some colour into the game, I have started making my own Devons from the garden Mock Orange bush. This useful creature already has hollow stems. You just have to push out the pith, saw the stem to size, shape it, paint it, and mount it on stiff nylon with beads and a treble. Painting was, naturally, in the approved colours of Colonel H. S. Crow, some time departed and much lamented by those who saw the military rasp as a desirable thing in the day of the punk. Incidentally, the colonel's book *Hampshire Avon Salmon* is a masterly, simple work which can be read between setting the alarm clock and turning out the light, and you should read it again every other night.

So, blue and gold it was, and borne to the river in late May like a talisman. If you are going to take your stand on luck, then try everything, but read Colonel Crow first.

This attack began like all the others. Start at the top of the beat and work down at the rate of three regulation paces per cast. The only thing to touch the brain is a decision about weight of lead, and while that might be a critical decision, the permutations are scarcely endless. I had on three-quarters of an ounce, which lifted quite sensibly over the weed bars and kissed the gravel in the deeps.

The first hour passed swiftly among the buttercups – the first hour of any kind of fishing always does that. In salmon fishing, though, it's how you measure up to the second hour that counts. If you find yourself thinking about what should be done about that matter festering away on the office desk, then things are going wrong. In other words, you are not angling, you are standing on a river bank chucking lead and bits of Mock Orange bush into the water like a nitwit.

For me, on this day, everything happened in that second hour. And the crowds gathered. Well, four people (though one had a camera), and as I hope I've indicated pretty clearly, my salmon fishing is not on beats graced only by distant figures in Norfolk jackets.

The first thrill was a couple of jags and a bit of a rush from a pike. That's another thing about Devons, they offer the chance of hooking pike when the salmon aren't around. And if anyone feels like sneering at "only a pike" then he shouldn't be reading this book. The pike came off because he was chomping on the minnow and not on the treble.

I continued the slow march, casting across and down with the Sharpe's cane, a nice performer. It's not a salmon rod but their heavy carp rod (*circa* 1965) never used for carp fishing, though, since carp can be even more trying than salmon. The line was 10 lb b.s. That's about half the strength recommended by the experts for spring, but since the reel was a fixed-spool and not a multiplier, thicker line won't rest easy in it. The trace was 9 lb b.s.

The fish took in a far bank glide and the cane met him very late, but well.

When you haven't hooked a salmon for a long time you make certain of contact by letting him have a second dragging pull to set the hooks. Then you come upon an important discovery which is that any concerns there may be in other parts of your life no longer exist for the duration of the battle.

Of course, you don't know how long the battle will last, but 7 lb of pull (allowing for wet strength at the knots of a 9 lb trace) is really quite a powerful matter. As I have said, though, people seeking 25-pounders among granite slabs would think my tackle too light for common sense.

I had no fears as he bored upstream, accelerated downstream, and then thrummed away below for a time. There was no question of a tug-of-war but even if 9 lb b.s. doesn't allow for that I really wasn't worried about the nylon.

Feeling in control of matters is an illusion which| all-season salmon fishers do not indulge in. I realised this with some force when I found that this part of the river was deep and my tailer rather short. I walked him up like a dog doing heelwork on the lead. He grew tired. The tailer sprang on some nettles. I reset it. The watchers in the meadows stirred uneasily then – not that I was aware of it at the time. Tailers are the price you pay for squeamishness I suppose, but I never use a gaff. Apart from the problems of kelts, I don't like putting holes in fish.

After a while, all this fiddling about gave my chap his second wind and he forged around some more, solid shoulders just breaking the surface before another dive. I walked him up for the third time, still looking for a suitable place to slip the wire on his wrist. In the strong current I could only just manage to hold him steady, but he remained way below the surface and impossible to lift. It was as I knelt to perform the tailing operation that my reel fell off. This time I was aware of the gallery because they all muttered in a tense way. All credit to them – they could have laughed. I did.

Here was this stout salmon fisher with his rod in a deadly kind of arc, scrabbling on his knees for the reel and trying to reset the tailer for the third or fourth time. Carp rods, of course, do not have screw reel fittings, but sliding ones.

There is no doubt at all that I deserved the aching right forearm as the fish fell back downstream, feebly aslant. This is the moment I do not not like, the wet-sack-of-cement feel, the water resistance, the lack of contact and trying to get below a fish as he shakes his head. Finally, he was close to the bank and quiet again. It all came together in a moment. The noose tightened in the right place, then the straight heave and backward stride from the water, and there he was, a fine fellow – fat and glinting on the grass. The priest fell, and I looked up at a ring of faces and congratulations which were well-meant though not well-earned.

That fish wasn't one for the record books. He weighed 17 lb, but I loved him. The home-made Devon was mounted in a glass-fronted box on the wall at home – an eccentricity which pleases me and is a lot cheaper than doing the same thing to a fish.

I take it all back – you can't beat the catching of salmon. The trembling goes on for a long time afterwards and sustains you through the next two seasons at least. When I came home clutching the fish in both hands, my wife said I looked like a smirking schoolboy.

CHAPTER FOUR

On special service

Don't tell me . . . I know that fishing is getting over-specialised. That hobby horse has been ridden once or twice in this book. During the last coarse season I only just managed to escape with my virtue intact. Apart from certain boffins in reservoir-land who catch more fish than other people, damn 'em, the problem doesn't seem to have reached trout fishing. Perhaps the gamey men are individuals who don't go in for group therapy or group think-tanks. Instead, each one believes he's a complete specimen group already.

Coarse fishing used to be like that and I think it was better then. A reactionary thought for this decade is that it was nicer when each man hugged his supposed secrets to himself and only passed them on in his will.

I hold to the old and forgotten virtues of angling. I cling to them in much the same way as I once clung to a tree growing over a Thames weir-pool after the dinghy I was in had been gripped rather hard, minutes after I lost the oars.

What are these virtues? They're to do with wonder and mystery. They arouse ancient lines like, "There's more to fishing than catching fish." They suggest you angle with constant hope rather than vicious dedication. And the result of this laughable attitude is delight at catching anything and gratitude for anything large. But as I said, at the end of last season the old virtue was threatened. I was *approached*.

I had often wondered how it happens; being *approached* doesn't occur to everbody. Imagine me – cane rod, willow basket and not a set of plastic-drainpipe rod-tubes in sight, and imagine this bloke suddenly materialising from the trees, so that I jumped and spilled half a tin of elderly maggots over my spool of 4x. (Yes, I said 4x, not 3¾ lb b.s.) He emerged, as I said, then fell upon one knee in a worshipping position. "Kinky", I muttered.

He didn't hear me and a closer look revealed that he was merely doing the angling move known as "keeping out of sight of the fish". I went on fishing for dace for a time, and was just thinking that I might change the float to something more artistic, when he spoke.

"Changing the float?" he asked.

"Yes", I said, "for something more artistic."

His mouth dropped to the first popper stud on his imitation para tunic. He stood up.

Nervously, I looked him over to see where he kept his grenades and Czech-made automatic. All he had was a revolutionary expression on his face.

"Are you going to be here long?" he asked.

"No."

"Good."

"Why?"

"Our group's moving in soon", he told me.

I knew what he meant, instantly. I didn't think he was a conservationist on litter-collection duties. I knew he was a specimen-hunter. You can tell, you see. At that point I was only in danger of getting angry but as I had people ringing, some work to do, and was going away that afternoon, it didn't seem worth it. So we talked and he turned into an ordinary bloke, like you and me.

We smoked and talked some more as I packed up. This must have made him very happy, because he told me that the English Record Barbel was waiting just a long trot-and-a-half downstream. He said it in capital letters as if expecting me to come to attention. Then he said he'd break the rule of The Group and show me.

Feeling unworthy, I listened as he said the fish was lying close-in under the bank down there. Then he gave me a platoon commander's overhead wave and set off across the meadow at right angles to the water. I fell into file as we did a big half-circle and got back to the river again. Then we dropped on our knees and had a conference.

The objective was made clear: the third thistle stalk on the left, between the fag packet and the buttercup.

"Put your head over the bank just there", he whispered, "and you'll see him."

On my belly I snaked through the grass. Since I weigh more than 13 stone, this is a kindly description. But I made it, and could hear his approval coming in grunts and whispers way behind. It was interesting to discover that between the fag packet and the buttercup was a large cow-pat. Now I know such things shouldn't matter, and that sinking my chin into the pat was probably expected of me, but I confess to moving half a slither to the left and peering over the bank from that position instead.

In the middle of a polaroid halo I saw two barbel, a big one and a small one. They were lying behind a boulder and looked ready to launch a dozen missiles at any moment. But they didn't look like The English Record – not even both together.

"Wadderyoureckon?" he asked, as I crawled back to his boots before rising.

"Dunno, but maybe four pounds and ten pounds."

"Two fish!" he said, with a look of interest, pulling out a notebook and writing something in it.

By now I could see his men coming across barbed wire in the distance. They seemed to be making good use of the country and kept disappearing into folds in the ground.

My interrogator said that if I was right about the big one they probably wouldn't bother. After all, reasonably well-confirmed reports had reached their intelligence service about one bigger than 10 lb only a short drive away. It was then that I got the offer.

"We're all barbel men", he said. Then he hesitated. I looked impressed and he made his decision.

"Look, you're a local", he went on. "What about being our Official Spotter down here?"

Perhaps I should have been modest and said that I had too many heavy responsibilities already. Perhaps I should have said I was too fond of fishing to sign up and take the oath. Instead I felt vaguely tempted. Presumably you can work for promotion in a group and get to hold a rod in the end. But the matter was taken out of my hands. As the others got closer he looked kind of nervous, mumbled something like "See you", and hurried away to meet them.

I think it was guilt about showing me the barbel. Serves him right, but I hope that nothing happens to him if they find out.

CHAPTER FIVE

The bronze age of leisure

There seems to be very little point in worrying about what they are doing to us in this age of leisure. They gave us a dye to turn maggots bronze which colours our hands like the heaviest chain-smokers that ever were, not to mention the possibility of cancer for our bladders. People who gave up fags and went fishing were still in the shadow of Big C, or that's what concerned people and commentators said.

Others laughed, like men who know that if one thing doesn't get you another will, and went on winning matches with gentles fed on chrysiodine. But the worry was there, niggling away, and it may be that by the time anybody reads this everybody will be playing safe.

Then there is the great lead shot row. We had lead centuries ago, so nobody can blame that on modern times, but we are told it is killing swans and polluting the environment. Never mind the human sewage or fields heavy with complex fertilisers; never mind all the leaks from the waste-maker society or the great gulps taken from our rivers by houses and industry – lead shot is polluting the environment.

Well, perhaps it is. And it may be that by the time somebody reads this we shall be playing safe and loading our floats with putty. Shall we think that is an advance? Does that mean everything will be all right now? At least the swans will only have shotgun fall-out or overhead power lines to worry about.

The time for getting worried, or just plain scared, is not now. It was years ago. As the acid rain falls on the just, the unjust and Friends of the Earth alike, most people know that the villains are not men in white coats or cackling capitalists without conscience, not tackle dealers selling lead and bronze. They are us.

The time to worry was when the population figures started rising from 43 million between the wars, to something like 56 million plus yesterday. But even in the 1940s it was too late. As a rather thoughtful chap called Professor Joad once said, if you want quality of life (he didn't actually say that, because it's a modern phrase, but that's what he meant) for all, then the best population level for Britain is about 6 million.

Even in a population of 6 million, bronze dye could still be nasty stuff – or not, as the case may finally turn out to be. As could lead and agrichemicals. But it is beyond doubt that there would be less of it all. Less muck and more space, fewer anglers and better fishing, less leisure pressure to accommodate and administrate.

Anybody who imagines that I'm just a selfish simpleton, turning an argument into a diatribe just because I want a mile of river to myself wherever I go, at all times, even on a summer Sunday, is perfectly correct. Except that I'd like *you* to have that as well, and you, and the men with the electron microscopes burning up computer time.

We may need these people because we have put ourselves into such a state that they must keep getting up to all sorts of tricks and producing all sorts of new things, just so that we won't stop and think about what we've lost or what might have been. Yet, in these times, that is not the danger. Our cry, now, is "What are they going to do for us?"

There's a limit to the amount of progress you need when the hunting instinct is sublimated to pure pastime and pleasure. After all, if you're hungry you'll put aside the bow for the rifle and telescopic sight, or aim a trolley at the shelves in the supermarket. Whatever anybody tells you, there must be a limit to advances in angling, just as there must be limits to economic growth. If there aren't, then everything will just split and sag tomorrow, or next month – if it doesn't go bang.

Meanwhile – and since we aren't going to bother with worrying about things – what's the latest way to make us think that fishing is getting better and better for more and more fishermen? After all, something will have to be done, because you can't have an age of leisure if everyone notices that the leisure won't fit in anywhere because all the others are after it too.

The answer seems to be to remember what anglers like best. All non-anglers in laboratories know what that is. It's big fish. Bigger and bigger fish all the time. Give us those and we'll be happy to leger in a washing machine, provided it contains a 20 lb carp.

So the helpful people battling to fill all the spare hours that come with flexitime, job-sharing, shorter working weeks and unemployment (and turning an honest penny while they're at it) have been doing clever things with fish genetics. What do you say – they've been doing that since the trout pellet? Indeed they have, and probably the monks round the manorial pond had a go, too . . . but there weren't enough of them to make much difference.

A news story in the papers says that mutant super carp can now be produced. In future, the men of science will be able to guarantee that every carp in the lake, pond or pail will be over 20 lb in weight. Now there's a happy thing! But even if the report is wrong it can't be long before something happens to ensure that tomorrow's angler gets good value for his £20 day ticket as he hurries through to the place set apart for communing with nature. They've done such clever things with trout for every table in every city, so why not for carp? Of course, as a consequence, we don't value the trout any more; but you can't have everything.

In a club newsletter I read some stern words covering hurt feelings about the private ways of carp fishers and how they don't like giving information to up-and-coming youngsters. It's all those secret baits they make, I think. A member of a sailing club which, under the new rules for sharing scarce watersport facilities, occupies a section of a certain lake, told me how he came across one of these hunched carp fishers on a quiet morning.

The angler turned up the collar of his denim jacket and gave an alarmed grunt when the sailor said something old-fashioned like "Good morning". His left hand did a kind of nervous jump and placed a fruit-pie packet over a small plastic container. Of course, he may not have been a real carp fisher at all but a company scientist diversifying from catfood and on the verge of a breakthrough. Perhaps he thought that the dinghy might sail off and spread the news of what was in that plastic box all round the lake.

Quite soon, now, all this secrecy will be quite unnecessary because the market is going to take care of things for us. A researcher has discovered that carp anglers are getting edgy because of all the competition. He has run off to the laboratory and told his colleagues about the problem. Before long, he reports, tense anglers will be breaking up the furniture or voting Labour. So Government money has been released to him and he now has thoughts of a Nobel prize.

The latest mutation probability may produce carp not of 20 lb but of 40 lb, and each fish will have two mouths. The mouth on the left will only feed on secret baits containing a safe bronze dye. But the mouth on the right will take only traditional bread-crust, bread-flake or worms.

I think I read this as a leak to the *Fish Farmers' Gazette*. Or if I didn't, then I soon will.

The first good fish I ever caught, and still the nicest I've ever seen, was a three-spined stickleback lurking mysteriously in a suburban park pond. It was red-throated, bold and big, and nobody had been monitoring its breeding procedures. I caught it by hand. I was eight.

The second good fish I remember was in a rather larger place, where real anglers sometimes went. It was a small roach and I took note of his dark cross-hatched back as he darted round the bottom of a green tin next to a man's folding canvas seat. Asked what it was, he said "Livebait". I didn't know about livebait, but I'd heard about whitebait. So I was rather puzzled about this name. When the angler bent down and took the fish from the tin I thought he was going to show it to me. When he stuck treble hooks all over it and cast it out under a big, red, round float, I was appalled. The chap had a small beard and reminded me of the devil. At no time in the next forty years did I ever use livebait.

After that I always had trouble in deciding what a good fish meant – or a good fishing day, come to that. You can't, or shouldn't, depend on big moments arriving every time. And those moments in the park and in the bait tin were big. I mean, *big*. It's going to take something pretty dramatic to match them.

Of course, I've never caught a 20 lb carp, otherwise I might be turning up my coat collar with the rest of them or, what is worse, looking forward to science making the next session worthwhile for me once more.

CHAPTER SIX

Mighty weapons for real men

It hasn't been easy to forget the day I saw the strangest sight in modern angling. A matter of counting the shudders, I suppose, and hoping.

There was this canal towpath. You went along it in a kind of jig, stepping round people who looked like bollards spaced at regular intervals for miles. To them no ships came to rest, but washed past in muddy scum. To them small fish came, once called tiddlers – which is a name lost in the past, when nobody thought of putting them in keepnets.

In the distance you could see a kind of black pimple perched on the end of a crane arm. As you walked along the path, the pimple became an intense kind of person on the end of a glass fibre pole. That was my first experience of what has, of course, become the most fashionable way of reaching out to the fish and casting a long shadow over the results columns.

This was obviously a confirmed poleman. He had over-developed tattooed biceps and something pretty lumpy by way of dorsal muscles. All this may or may not have compensated for the slipped disc he was heading for if he kept up this form of fishing.

Much later I had a pole of my own, and I never want to see another. But perhaps that's the result of failure to exercise properly. I had it for a few weeks and used it only twice. During that time I dismissed crude thoughts about a man's performance being judged by the length of his weapon (actually there's some truth in that symbolism among polemen, but never mind) and just thought that someone had to make a stand somewhere. We all have enough weaponry and it's only fish we're after. Why go in for overkill?

My pole came to me as a prize in a fishing match. It was a big green telescope with red plastic ends and some Italian name just above the red plastic hand-grip. At first, the idea that it was purely for red plastic people, puffing and heaving, did not occur to me. With this (I thought) it would surely be possible to encompass vast reaches of river and lake. With this I could strike shy fish in but a turning-over of the wrist. With this I could follow a matchstick float into new realms of sensitivity and efficiency.

A bit of the charm still clung to things during the preparation period. There was a wire crook to learn about and the mystery of fine elastic. There was a whole new range of "continental" polefloats to puzzle over, and weights in any shape but round. Then the stance had to be practised. Of course, you couldn't put the thing down unless you had bought, or made, a particular kind of rod-rest or, rather, a hoop-of-steel rod-gripper. In all this I consoled myself with traditional pictures of ancient Lea roach fishers whose poles were of hardwood and whalebone, while mine sprang from modern technology. If they did well and with artistry, surely I could do better and with less effort.

In fact I've just remembered that this was really my second experience of polemanship. Years ago (it must have been the fifties) something called "The Japanese Roach Pole" reached London. Well, perhaps it really got no further than one shop in the London suburbs, and just as well. It was all bamboo, and knobbly with it. Each section was tipped with brick-red paint and there was a silken loop

on the fine end of the top joint. That one went to the back
of the garage after I tried to plumb the depths of the River
Medway and the pole bent double under the strain.

Anyway, the green telescope was different. Put a
plummet on and you couldn't feel a thing. Put a fish on
and you couldn't, either. In the angling magazines it said
that everybody with a pole was doing better than before
they had a pole. But, they added gravely, this only applied
to those who put up at least 9 metres when they got to the
water. Anything less and you weren't really in with a
chance.

It always takes me some time to understand metres,
but since mine was something like 6 of them, and that's
something more than 6 yards to the undecimalised, I felt
it was a mighty weapon indeed. Then I came across a rather
interesting sensation.

Erecting everything beside a gravel pit, I realised that
even 6 metres didn't give me titantic feelings. Compared
with the far bank, I didn't seem to be reaching out as far
as I thought I might. The pole seemed to go much farther
when I was playing with it in the garden beforehand. Good
heavens, the thing was too short! The magazines were right:
I needed a longer pole. Then I read another article which
said (sternly, this time) that real men handled nothing less
than 12 metres. A wave of emasculation came over me,
but I fought back.

The important slice of knowledge that came to me by
that gravel pit was that even 6 metres of glass fibre is about
as lively as the arm of a crane. After just two casts or, if
you like, lumbering swings, I knew I was never going to
be an ancient Lea roach poleman. Sensitivity? A turn of
the wrist? Flicker and flash?

All I got was a kind of yawing, creaking floppiness
and three small bream which felt like leaves blowing in the
wind. The pole just leaned down a little more as if forcing
itself to make the gesture.

No doubt some polemen can cast into a stiff breeze without feeling as if they are beating a carpet – German floats, wire crooks, French elastic and all. Perhaps they are also able to work out the mathematics involved in fixed line versus varying depths all having to equal a manageable distance between pole tip and float tip. I could have done it myself with pencil, paper and patience. The trouble was, I realised, that it hardly seemed worth the effort. I wasn't fishing the pole, the pole was fishing me. If only it could have found a fulcrum it would have moved the world, or at least lifted me off my basket with no trouble at all. However, since fulcrums don't often come floating by, the pole could do nothing but bear down on knee and forearm with a sullen sag, stirring only to the breeze as it passed, when all the strength in my failing wrists was needed to keep it steady.

Though all this is quite true, the decision to dispose of the green pole was taken with regret. Not for the object itself, but at my failure with it. Thousands of polemen couldn't be wrong. They were catching fish and, presumably, enjoying it. But it's how you catch them that counts and if tackle is part of the matter, then it should feel right in the scale of things.

Yet it must be admitted that an ordinary twelve- or thirteen-foot rod does seem like a mere pencil after the pole. Switching from pole to rod you forget that fixed-spool reels have been invented and think of your fishing as a mere pecking at the edges. The feeling soon wears off if you have given up the pole pretty quickly – though the logic of the tight line still nags away at the back of your mind.

Perhaps that's why I took the pole to an obliging tackle shop and swopped it for a second-hand Irish Monster. This one comes in its own kitbag, every inch of which is needed. It's in four sections, black with shamrock whippings. When assembled it stretches to eighteen Irish feet and on the butt is a transfer which says ''Guaranteed Irish''. As a matter of fact it is really a pole with rod rings and reel seating. I pass over the jokes about how this rod was made to catch blundering bogfish, because it gives me length without that abominable elastic.

With the Monster you don't have to wonder how the virtue of keeping a tight line may be squared with the sudden surprise of an 8 lb bream or a 14 lb carp on the end, and no reel in sight. But it's ugly, bedad, it's awful ugly. Creaking and flopping, just like the pole, the Irish Monster frightens the swans and casts a mighty shadow – except at high noon, when it seems merely to wilt in the sun and lean lower towards the water.

In a wild, experimental moment I tried trotting with it on a fast river swim. With a centrepin reel it did give perfect float control, everything in line behind the cane and balsa, precisely one foot of monofil on the water astern of the float and an instant, sweeping strike made without line belly to take up.

Well, a sweeping strike can be made in this ideal way once, twice . . . even thrice. Indeed, you can go on summoning up striking power for about an hour on the Hampshire Avon. If you use two hands, that is. After that, you haven't the strength to impale a single maggot on the hook because your hands won't operate your fingers.

I very much doubt if even the huskiest Irishmen are ever seen with the Monster. Of course, it must have been designed for stillwater work. They probably strap themselves to it with webbing harness and fish all day in a contemplative manner like long-beaked herons in a Celtic mist.

A good time for thinking up more strange things to export to the English who, as is well known, will buy anything.

CHAPTER SEVEN

Doomwatching the generation gap

You are not up to date if all you take to the water are swim feeders in six shapes, foaming groundbait lozenges, soluble plastic bags (also for groundbait), swing, spring and quiver tips, hypodermic syringes for aerating worms, beta-lights, and packets of coloured powder from France: that lot's no good at all unless you add the latest invention – the DIY filth-measurement outfit, otherwise known as the Doomwatch Kit or even PTE (Pollution Testing Equipment).

So far, these kits aren't common in the tackle shops. They cost about 75 pence when I first heard of them. They were largely in the hands of schoolchildren, then, and I am surprised that they haven't yet become right little pests with them. Youngsters are being taken to rivers by their teachers, who reckon that angling should be made a GCE subject. Indeed, it may be one by now.

So, one minute you're quietly trotting a gilt-tail and the next minute there's a bankside buzzing of bespectacled boffins, loaded with PTE. Progressive anglers, like progressive teachers (I never could understand either of them), show delight at having so much enthusiasm around. This fades rapidly.

"Grayling are the first to go", says a wizened eleven-year-old with a fistful of wet litmus paper.

His twelve-year-old mate (laboratory monitor as well as the owner of the microscope) adds happily: "We've found something nasty in your river, mister."

You gulp and gnaw the end of your wire-stemmed float as a trendy, semi-adult voice pipes up from the back of the crowd: "It's fourth-degree pollution, guys, and we've proved it." Since that was the science master, you have to take note.

The only thing to do, really, is learn from them. Buy yourself some PTE (it came from Cambridge originally, I think) and get a famous angler to condemn it as likely to frighten the fish. If that doesn't work, get all the ban-happy club secretaries to remember the great hempseed controversy and suggest that these kits are a definite hazard. Fish are becoming preoccupied with litmus paper and won't look at maggots or coloured French powder any more.

Failing that, we could play clever, and adopt the kits as the bright competitor's secret weapon. One man I know, but refuse to speak to, has worked out plans to use them as a ploy in biggish matches. What you do, he says, is break the water with a test tube rather than with groundbait as soon as the whistle blows. Don't tackle up, don't lay out your stand of maggot boxes, don't even put in your rod rests. Just take water samples and look grave. A little later you look even graver. Lay out the equipment on top of your seat box and ponder over it.

After a time, all the others – who are busily splashing in groundbait of various colours – will notice that you don't seem to have their degree of dedication. When their curiosity is sizzling, you stand up. Then you give a wild shriek. Then you stride off, shouting for a steward.

On the way past the other pegs you babble about a wave of pollution eddying round your peg and spreading all through your section. Even show them the litmus paper, which proves it. This scatters a most satisfactory state of panic around and the effect on morale could be most useful to you.

All you have to do then is carry out another test ten minutes later, with the baffled steward watching. Then announce that your peg is now clear, but you don't know where the stuff's gone. Then you start fishing in earnest and refuse all pleas to borrow your PTE from those who are getting no bites.

After a season of this you should find the NFA voting on the subject. Following the inevitable row, a general ban will be issued and that should clear away the menace for ever. When you have a nice clean river, you don't want anyone spoiling the illusion. And kids are there to be taught, not to make you feel uneasy.

The great thing though, is to be in the swim, to know what's going on. There's no excuse for ignorance these days since it's the age of instant communication as well as of precocious children.

They were weed-cutting on my local river. I admit that, even in the age of mass communication, the water authority hadn't told me . . . which is just as well since I'd have told them not to do it, because weed is good for fish. And they wouldn't have listened, which would have caused bad feeling.

Anyway, there was this littered stream. Bundles and rafts of weed were coming down, and even in the gaps there were snaky pieces at all levels, seeking to snatch the line.

Long trotting had given way to short trotting and then to legering close to the bank. Finally, I packed up and went to a gravel pit down the road where, in the heat of the day, I watched a float that I knew would never move, even when shotted with great cleverness. In the heat of the day, few floats are seen to move on gravel pits, and none does anything so energetic as diving away.

As the sun glowed on the water, we Sunday afternoon idlers basked under our Wimbledon eyeshades. Thin antenna floats were pencil marks on shiny paper. Our swing tips looked like pieces of angle-iron in the harsh reflection, and behaved like that too. It was an immobile time.

The striped, folding picnic chairs made a holiday scene, along with the wives reading steaming paperbacks, or Mills and Boons which dispense gentler heat. Dogs scratched and slept. The unusual thing was the essential calmness of it all. This scene was not for the children of our times – which means all of us, usually – who are plugged into the latest developments and live high on expectation. If desire is unfulfilled, then just flick the switch again.

Much as the world owes us a living, so the pit owes us fish. And they must not be ordinary fish, because we read in the angling papers that people are catching special-category bream. A bream of 4 lb is not worthwhile. "What did you get?" Only small stuff, but Wayne had an "8" and Gary dropped a "6".

But nobody said anything like that on this creaking old man's Sunday. Nobody got out his PTE just for the sake of creating a stir and livening everybody up. Some had come a long way and were going back that evening, but they sat on hopefully – stripped to the waist to catch a tan, if nothing else.

Were they unplugged? Detached, just for this afternoon, from the need to deliver, to succeed, to earn their due for the outlay on petrol and maggots? Even relieved from the burden of wondering why the fish weren't feeding? To that we must say yes, each time. Most of the anglers round that pit were over thirty, which may mean something. And some were over forty, which may mean a lot and not all of it praiseworthy. But there you are.

In the car park there was a sudden movement. Action. Loud voices. Great laughter with a harsh edge. Today's music came from a radio and jabbed at yesterday's foxgloves.

Yet there was no laughter in these faces as they stuck rod-bags under hatchbacks and hitched up their jeans for departure. No, they weren't packing up, mate. Not really. Not so as you'd notice. Going to get some fish, weren't they? Had enough of this place. At another place they knew you were charged £5 a day for the certainty of fish. Stocked it was, they said. Full of big bream it was, and tench, nothing under "4". And roach. Only a small pond, but you couldn't miss.

The leader-figure bashed his accelerator several times as the tribal cars fell into line. Then they left in a spurt of gravel and a haze of dust which put a fine gritty coating all over the generation gap.

Maybe that's all it is, after all. Maybe the only change is the passage of years, and experience is knowing that all the clichés are true. I hoped that when their cars invaded that pond they could stay on into the evening and catch an "8". Or at least a "6".

Since nobody talks about garden canes, twine and bent pins any more, it is easy to think that people have altered when all that has happened is that *you* have.

When a small nephew came in as I was rummaging in tackle drawers, he didn't ask to see my PTE. I gave him a couple of floats, though. He is a lad weaned on video games and stereo sound, but his voice dropped reverentially. He bore the floats away quietly, in cupped hands, as if holding holy water. At his age, I behaved in the same way when somebody gave me a float. I arranged it in an old cigar box among cotton wool in case its paint got scratched.

Despite all we do to rush him, the boy is still closer to the ground than the man. He will see the lizard in the bracken while you walk above with the worries of the world or the fear that tomorrow's test with the PTE will be for real – and prove positive.

CHAPTER EIGHT

A spell on virgin water

There's only one thing wrong with our home river. It doesn't seem to have many secret places – at least, not getattable secret places.

There are some remarkable disorientating loops. There are shallows and deeps, eddies below bridges, happy shallow straights and some pretty imposing broad reaches. Its weirs, while not large, do roar quite well, at least in winter. But sometimes you feel like a change.

Change to other places, though, and you find that they've lost their nooks and crannies too. Their sidestreams have been dried out and their water meadow systems lost for ever. If you want a sad fact of life, then it is that there are very few farmers these days who are still sitting on fishable water which has never seen a rod. I would say that there are *no* farmers left with that kind of water, but I don't because – as the old boys taught us – the words "always" and "never" do not apply to angling.

Sometimes it's good to put aside thoughts of mighty fish in well-known places – or big bags on standard match stretches – for the sake of seeking smaller fry in odd little places. If you measure achievement by packing in the bream after moving a dust shot three inches closer to the hook, and winning the big match then, yes, granted you've changed things in the modern manner and congratulations are due, and sincerely offered.

But isn't it more fun to beat the lesser waters? When you move to them you change your habitat and that is an achievement. But you only feel like this if, on balance, your surroundings matter more than your amibition and you value the quality of surprise.

When a river scout reported to our local club that he'd got us an unknown stream his voice dropped and took on ethereal tones. "It's virgin water", he said. There's nothing quite like those words. They are probably the most dramatic that can be presented to worldy-wise anglers. Jaded appetites revive and you recapture that feeling, so fragile and so underrated, of going fishing for the first time.

Virgin water it was. In places a ditch, in others a stream. Virgin water also means that it is full of tree trunks, silt, reeds, a bull in the meadow and a marsh everywhere else. In other words, ideal, old-fashioned fishing. On this stream you could squelch through the mud and might expect to see milkmaids on three-legged stools over the other side of the hedge.

My first visit renewed old pleasures. No, not of chatting up milkmaids – but of not being able to find the water. If you missed a fold in the ground, you missed the little stream. If you made a detour to avoid the bull – which always seemed to be standing over the most fishable area – then you couldn't pick up the flow of things again. In the end, though, you find a green tunnel and think of boyhood. In the end (and I hope this has happened to you), there's a happy little waterway waiting.

So I settled down in a thicket at the corner of a field, by a wall covered in moss. The brickwork had obviously been part of some grand structure in distant days, perhaps a footbridge spanning the stream, which was all of ten feet across. But there it was that the butterflies of boyhood came to brush against my ears. Nettles stung with reminders of dockleaves and bees hummed with reminders of blue-bags.

It was a place of sunshine on old brick, heat on the knees, and not a sound from road or sky. Just me and the stream.

As far as the matter of fishing goes, you must, of course, use cane in such places, resting your rod on the ground or in a forked twig cut from the bush with an ivory-handled knife handed down through the family – and with very thin blades. I broke off a bit of dead branch instead, but at least the thought was there. My cheap Pakistani imitation of the famous American ''bear claw'' knife doesn't cut very well.

There could be no suggestion of using a float. The shining and steady trickle was no depth at all in front, where the stream bed rose to make a resting-place for grey wagtails. At other points in the swim it was still shallow, but round the bend a little, below a clump of weed and near a tangle of branches, it looked as if we had a deep hole by the standards of the place. It was all a matter of scaling-down – tackle, attitude and expectations. Delicate work was needed. Really a quiver tip should have been used, but cane rods don't have tip rings with screw fittings, at least mine haven't. And, since we aren't expected to use cane rods any more, I imagine nobody else's has, either.

On with a centrepin reel, then, for the sake of the past. Load it with 2 lb b.s. and arm the line with a size 18 hook. Two feet from the hook, pinch on one AA shot. I am ready for the virgin water. A gentle cast so that the single maggot swung into the hole downstream. I thought that there might be a fat gudgeon there and some roachlings, if there was anything at all.

Then everything happened with a zing. The line jerked, the rod tip banged and a trout sprang out. No need to strike. He hooked himself and danced all over the place. He was bright and hard and about half a pound. When I put him back he shot off downstream behind a bow wave. So I lit a pipe and waited for things to calm down.

The next bite was indeed a fat gudgeon, and the next. There followed a perch of three inches – and five more – and some minnows who flicked the rod tip as if they were knocking at a door on a neighbourly visit.

At some point during this sweet day a minnow knocked and my small answer had me shaking at the wrist to a great pull and jerk. The fish felt unstoppable. I can still remember the sense of surprise as I played the chub. He weighed 3 lb and though I have had heavier chub, none has seemed bigger.

It is, I think, a mistake to believe that out-of-the-way places mean that the fish in them are anxious to give themselves up. On that little stream though, quiet methods, a simple approach and keeping out of sight, ensured that the fishing wasn't difficult.

But let me tell you that the same success didn't come in another spot. Not from the Witch's Pool, it didn't. There, everything was baffling. This was the smallest pond which could be considered as an angling water. The next stage down would be for gnomes. It was right in the middle of thistles, bracken and blasted heath. You either walked by within inches without seeing it, or you fell in; there was no third course of action – like spotting it from afar or finding it on a map.

I only know it was called the Witch's Pool because that's what a boy who looked like William Brown said. For those who don't know William Brown, it is enough to say that he was not thought to exist any more. Obviously his descendants aren't all stuck in front of the telly, after all.

He noticed my rod and said: "You going down the Witch's Pool?" I supposed that I was. "Just been there, me", he said. Then he did a kind of Rumplestiltskin jump, grinned wickedly and said: "Never seen no-one fishing in it before."

Then he disappeared. Just like that. Not uncannily, like a witch's familiar, but like a boy with so much else to do.

The pool was almost perfectly circular, almost entirely cupped in rushes and almost entirely green. This was due partly to reflection from the reeds and partly to duckweed growth. There was just one clear gash in all this greenery where the water looked deep and black. One fishable spot, never fished – not even by William Brown and his gang.

So I fished and caught nothing but I kept missing bites. On the second visit, in the early morning, the same thing: bite, miss, bite, miss. Fishing in the late evening there was a repeat performance. I used light floats. I used mere dust shot. After many hours, just one middling roach came to the net; yet it seemed worth persevering, because I just touched something for an instant and it didn't feel like a stickleback. It looked as if nothing on the bottom, under the surface or at mid-water could get them to close their mouths long enough to be hooked. Fishing "on the drop" was no good either. The slowly sinking bait yielded short pull-away bites with nothing on the end of them.

As I was packing up in the evening light I thought I heard a strange cackle behind the reed fringe, but it was probably just William on his way home.

No, I didn't give up. But from then on it was secret recipe and cranky reasoning time. The problem, as it seemed to me, was to present a slow, sinking bait which allowed contact with events while also letting the fish do a bit of chomping, even if only the keen ones would hang on.

I had given up on the casual nudges. Float and shot didn't work. The dough-bobbin leger showed a few unhittable movements but, anyway, I lost confidence in that method as the bottom was covered in silkweed.

One morning I took a long, whippy sea-trout rod to the pond, together with a certain amount of desperation. I had a bag of dust made from crushed trout-food pellets and the bait was boiled pellet mixture. Looking over my shoulder just in case people I know had decided to discover the pool at that moment, I then faced front, took a deep breath, and launched into the silly experiment.

Ever tried casting gooey paste with a fly rod? It has rather too much weight and rather too little adhesion. So you don't cast, you do a kind of ungainly sideswing. Then you look over your shoulder again. Surprisingly, though, once the lot hit the water the balance was just right.

A sinking flyline was out of the question in this little pond. So six feet of 2½ lb monofil was nail-knotted to an ordinary floating line. The line was the indicator and the weight of the paste sank the tip little by little. You could see the water closing over each inch of line as the smelly paste sank through its groundbait cloud.

The response was good. All that happened was that instead of the line sinking an inch or so at a time, you suddenly saw a foot of it draw under and you tightened rather than struck.

It was a small tench that broke the spell, then larger tench. I would like to say monster tench, but I don't feel the need – since they weren't, and I was happy with them anyway.

After a time the bites became stronger as the groundbait whipped up a bit more excitement down below. The flyline began disappearing in nice, slow draws and stocky little crucians began appearing among the tench and occasional roach. Then it sank in dramatic rushes. Then I began missing again. By that time the bites were travelling in big spasms right up to the rod tip and I was missing them all.

I went back to the Witch's Pool once or twice after that, but never again filled the keepnet. The old mystery had returned, and while I caught the occasional fish, it was obvious that I hadn't stumbled on the certain method for virgin water.

Either that, or the witch's spell had been recast and even stranger methods were now called for. But they will never be discovered. The blasted heath is now a housing estate.

CHAPTER NINE

Dressing the part

Forgetting the evil chuckle (elsewhere in this book) at the wearing of paramilitary costume on the river, you have to accept that camouflage is always a sensible study for the practical angler. But if you think that other things count almost as much, then I'll agree.

In all the years that lie behind, I recall perhaps no more than three or four original arbiters of angling fashion, and only one of them has stayed like that. He has never fished with anything but good tweed on his back and on his head; the only concession to the passing years has been the introduction of a woollen sweater (instead of a waistcoat) in deep winter. And that was a decision taken only after deep thought.

You won't find many these days who look like sepia photographs from the age of the blowline or cork-on-quill, so there's no danger of seeing a reversal of the trend in dresswear.

Don't think I'm making a push for elegance. After all, middle-aged men go to their offices these days in order to parade their deep joggers' chests before their secretaries. The macho medallion and the open-necked shirt are now part of our social history in the making and most anglers operate in mud and groundbait; at least they do before and after fly-fishing time.

However, it must be said that even fly fishers turn to the blue anorak or green vinyl tanksuit. If you see a figure who is decently dressed – or anciently dressed, if you like – then you feel guilty and wonder if you have your rod licence with you. He's either a keeper or the owner of the fishing.

For a while it looked as if the cult of the Barbour jacket would cover at least the worst sins. Sadly, these splendid garments can't resist barbed wire – and there's more barbed wire than hedgerow on the fishing scene nowadays. Smart proofed cloth can cope with groundbait stains and squashed maggots, but only if you clean it occasionally. Most of us don't even clean our reels very often, so a good jacket takes a lot of abuse as well. I suppose that only Sloane Rangers can be certain of appearing in public without looking mucky or tattered.

Incidentally, I re-proofed my jacket last season. You have to put a tin of wax in hot water and work long hours before you get that virtuous glow in the cloth and your soul. Now the coat looks so fine that I don't like to take it out – at least not to any old place. Perhaps I'll save it till I can afford a Range Rover.

But let's get down to sensible, practical matters. Which clothing is the best? What's good sense? And, if you care about such things, how do you cope with strange French stuff that most people seem to mix with their breadcrumbs, and the bream slime on top? The answer seems to be that you wear something so harsh and shining that we're all reminded of motorway repair gangs in the rain, rather than quiet folk in rural meadows.

What a bloke wears is nothing to do with me, because if I wince he'll not be allowed to notice; and if he frightens the fish he won't catch any, leaving more for the rest of us. It's a simple truth, nevertheless, that you are thought to be what you wear. Yes, even in fishing.

Why else should so many seekers after glory and confidence stick badges all round their hats, arms, backs, fronts and tackle boxes? This doesn't mark them out at all, because so many people do it. If you want to be noticed – and I can't imagine why you should – then go badgeless to the waterside. Or naked.

I will tell you what happened to me on a wooded stretch in Dorset where I sat (badgeless) after roach, in the rain, with breadcrumbs. If you want roach in that place you must fish hard against the far bank. It's 12 feet deep in the middle, but the fish like three or four feet of water below that far bank.

I'd put a peacock quill across and sunk the line to avoid wind drag. While craning round some reeds and squinting through a patch of sunlight which seemed to be following the slow passage of the float, I didn't notice that someone had joined me, with a hearty laugh of recognition. When I turned round, I saw a face from twenty years ago. He saw mine in the same way, but that wasn't what made him stop.

"I'd know that old coat anywhere", he said. "Knew it was you after all this time."

Here's where I confess that my contribution to bankside fashion – in winter at least – is an army greatcoat. What I hadn't realised was that the same coat had lasted me twenty years. There's worse to come: it was made for yesterday's Tommies, not today's yomping soldiers. So, when I bought it twenty years back, it was already destined for the Imperial War Museum.

Now, to be recognised by the cut of your threadbare army greatcoat may or may not be a compliment. All I can say is that when, a little while after, I won a club match (in a different place, but with roach, as it happened) the secretary who handed over a rather small number of notes said he reckoned I might now be able to afford a decent coat. Everybody laughed.

So I checked up on Old Faithful and found that it was thin on the shoulders after years of laceration by the strap of my willow basket, and I noticed that the collar was due for turning a second time, and that's impossible. Yet I solemnly affirm that in seeking another greatcoat like it I was doing the sensible thing. Even when rubbed bare, even with bullet holes, it still keeps out the rain and the cold.

The absorption quality of these old coats is remarkable. The water is held but just doesn't get through. Instead the cloth grows heavier by the hour. The collar turns up high about your ears. The pockets are large and the coat is long enough to reach below the knee and over rubber boots. What's more, it brushes clean with no trouble and, of course, khaki enables you to merge with the mud. In short, such a coat has it all. But before everybody is so impressed by my reasoning that they rush off to the Government Surplus Stores tomorrow – be warned that this is what I did, and I am still looking.

In the first place – and whatever the state of the army itself (pretty damn good) – army greatcoats are not what they were. For one thing, they seem to make them only for small people these days. Or, at least, for thin people, Still that could be merely that my shape has changed slightly over the last twenty years.

I asked various storemen in the back streets of England if they had an oversize British Army greatcoat, *circa* 1944, Dismounted Pattern. "Not a chance", they said. They meant not a chance on size, to start with and not a chance anyway, to finish with.

"We call you RSM size", they said.

I was unflattered. I was also depressed because, being observant, I'd noticed that the RSMs of today seem to be younger and smaller than I remembered them. Apart from the fact that modern khaki is a different shade from last-war or Great-War khaki, and not so good from the camouflage point of view, there's one major drawback waiting for the eager buyer – all the kids have been there first.

In case nobody's yet grasped the fact, I must tell you that Sloane Ranger Barbour is not the only fashion for non-angling layabouts. Young people have been wearing army greatcoats to posh parties, or discotheques, or wherever young people go in wintertime. They have cleaned out the surplus stores and pushed prices up. Worse, they have left the shopkeepers with no choice but to go to NATO. So all that's left on the racks is some flimsy foreign-looking stuff from Germany and Italy. You can get bright RAF blue which might be nice, but doesn't feel right when you're fishing. Roach are not specially impressed by Squadron Leaders or even the men who service Tornados, but they'll stomach a brown job, if he stays quiet.

For the moment, I've settled for the Civil Defence – not on grounds of dark blue but because the coat was just the right size. It was also new (no doubt there's a shortage of eager civil defenders), cheap, and of high quality.

Of course, fishing acquaintances no longer recognise me, but others think I am a public-spirited fellow. They must do, since they never want to know what I've caught but keep asking about the radiation level.

CHAPTER TEN

Leaves on a hot pond

A quiet angler nobody remembers now – which is probably as it should be, or he would have been a loud angler – thought up a title for his book: it was *Some Leaves on a River*. I've forgotten the book, but not the title. It's almost as good as that perfect title for a poetry anthology, *Other Men's Flowers*. But none of this is any help for keepers of fishing diaries.

Diary pages are indeed leaves on lake, pond or river but are far less substantial and not nearly as colourful as those that fall in autumn. Still, they are meant only for the writer. Of course, there are fishing diaries *and* fishing diaries. Some are a kind of secret romance with the Witchery of Water (another good book title, incidentally), a romance renewed on each page. Others are, I suppose, more like profit-and-loss accounts which the matchmen on the open circuit keep. These are even more secret than the other kind, and entirely sensible.

One day such diaries may interest historians as fringe examples of inflation in sport during this period. Travel to Long Barren Drain for practice session: £14.50. Travel to match: ditto, less petrol cost share: Wayne £3, Elvis £3, Darren £3, me £5.50 because I went to pick up the bait. 1½ gallons bronze maggots £15. Half gallon pinkies . . . hemp . . . beer . . . Then over to the winnings column, where eyes light up – or not – as the leaves turn.

My diary is practical, too – not about money but about water conditions and tackle. And it does obey the famous rule about diaries, which is that they should tell the truth, of course. Do you think that, in looking back to that day in 1984, you want to wonder if you exaggerated, now that you are due to fish that place again and want to get the method right this time?

To be honest, then, it must be said that the record of fourteen seasons' work with the rod is not a tale of continual improvement. If a schoolmaster got hold of the diary he'd write: "Could do better", in red ink. So it's the record of an average angler who just happens to have kept it up. But the pages prove all sorts of things – like how many blank days there were in 1972; like the effect of water temperature readings on the catching rate.

Doesn't that sound impressive? Here's a fellow who writes down the water temperatures every day he fishes – must be a scientific angler, after all. Don't you believe it!

Some thoughtful anglers of the past laboured over their water temperatures and, no doubt, many still do and are grand anglers in the present. We don't know if the thermometer is responsible for the grandeur, but are encouraged just the same.

If the only thing that stands between you and the men with the heavy keepnets is a few degrees Fahrenheit, then it's only necessary to go out and buy a thermometer. That's where I found some difficulty: water temperature thermometers don't grow on trees. They appear in magazine articles and books with impressive titles, but not in tackle shops. Well, not often. You have to search and you have to pay.

My first was the size of a fountain pen and had a clip for securing it to your pocket. "Not much call for these", said the dealer who unearthed it from a corner of the window normally kept for dead flies which had tried to make it from maggot room to freedom and found glass in between.

The thing didn't work. Not only would it fail to register 45 degrees (that's close to red-letter-day level, according to most temperature keepers) but it decided to stick for ever at 55 degrees. You could make the red line move above that if you tried hard, but there's no confidence to be found in that reading when the line is icing up in the rings. Anyway, I lost it after about a fortnight.

The tackle dealer looked in his window again, and in other corners, but not another thermometer could be found. So I went to a garden supplies shop and bought one with a rectangular plastic frame and a red line that moved up and down quite smartly. A few scientific entries were scribbled in as a result. Then a cow trod on it.

I persevered. Tackle dealers in other towns searched, and said there was no call for them. "What do you mean?" I said. "How can you be a modern scientific angler without a thermometer?" They all sighed and turned to serve other people. So I went right to the top, to a chemist who had letters after his name and three large catalogues in his drawer, each from a scientific thermometer specialist. "My diary needs you", I said.

The chemist spoke to me like one man of science to another. It was a little while before I realised that he thought I wanted to test the baby's bath-water. "My wife always used her elbow for that", I said.

When he found out that I wanted an instrument that would register, with perfect accuracy, cold water temperature from freezing to about 70 degrees, the pages of the catalogue moved for a long time and his finger stopped nowhere. "Not much call for that kind of thermometer", he said.

The best he could do was one that people buy after they have built themselves a swimming pool. When it arrived from the wholesaler its price was so high that I thought anyone who bought it *before* building a swimming pool wouldn't be able to afford the project. It's a foot long, in heavy chrome. With its retaining string attached to the rod-rest, it enters the water as if it was going on to bore a hole in the river bed. It hasn't helped me to catch more fish but it has given a scholarly air to the diary – well, it did for a few pages.

Now I hardly bother with the thing. The honest record of fishing days piled up certain evidence which I noted with a flash of considerable scientific insight. Whenever I wrote down the water temperature I seemed to have very little to say about the fish that were caught – for the simple reason that not many were. And when I did have something to write, it didn't relate to what the learned books say should have happened. Temperature is supposed to guide you to the species most likely to be feeding, and where, and the baits most likely to succeed.

Well, it probably does all those things for men with the intelligence to deduce correctly from the figures. But if you want my opinion, the chrome missile was frightening the fish. In with the thermometer as you tackle up; away with the fish before the first cast. No doubt that's why people weren't too happy to be pegged near me in our club competitions.

As it happens, another blinding truth hit me – some years after it had hit everyone else, including thermometer-makers and tackle-dealers. Since when did an angler go home without unpacking his kit, just because the thermometer said something depressing in degrees? If the reading is poor for the time of year all it can do is take away a bit of your confidence. Unfortunately it is well understood that if you don't fish with anticipation then usually you don't catch much. As the man said, there's no call for them. He must have meant that everybody was too busy fishing to bother, or swimming in their pools, come to that.

One of the most useful moments in the diary records not a day of bucking rod and mighty haul, but a time of crisis in the garden pond.

Incidentally, that pond could have been a swimming pool. When the JCB came in to lay a main sewer I persuaded the driver and his mate to take a break in order to dig me a big hole for a fiver.

"Each?" asked the driver, unearthing a third mate from behind a bush and adding that it was their lunch-time.

"Each", I said grandly.

The hole was dug before their tea got cold. What I can't remember (and the diary doesn't tell me) is whether I told my wife that it was going to be a swimming pool. Anyway, it was a hole that became a pond.

Over some years I'd been stocking the pond from angling trips and mentioning this only to my diary in case someone with a rule-book found out. Once a six-inch chub grew to nearly a pound and terrorised the neighbourhood until a heron got him. Minnows flourished (surprisingly), leaping for flies on warm evenings. Gudgeon carpeted the bottom – five minutes with a minnow trap proved it any day. Half a dozen one-inch carpling turned into stocky little chaps with grins on their faces. And dace played under the fountain.

The diary proved that everything in the pond was lovely for season after season. Indeed, sometimes it seemed that you could have a better day if you took your rod down the garden than if you went anywhere else.

On one occasion I did just that, when no-one was looking, because the minnows had disappeared and my diary told me that, in a stupid moment a year back, I'd put in two small perch. But the perch seemed to have gone, too, and all I caught was minnows after all . . . and a newt. He must have been the first palmate newt ever to enter a fishing diary.

The holocaust broke upon the pond one June. Two dead roach I didn't know I had were seen among the lilies.

Next day it was five gudgeon. Something was wrong, I thought, as I buried them in the compost heap. Now the struggle to save the fish from a de-oxygenated pond silted with grey mud was set down in ballpoint. As the fish came up gasping at the thin surface film mixed with alien chemistry, they were netted and put in an old tin bath, where they died.

The reason for their deaths after being rescued was water temperature. It's one thing fiddling about with thermometers in an attempt to catch more fish, but if a so-called angler doesn't know enough to save his pet fish, then he might as well give up keeping diaries. Of course, they were hoisted from a hot pond to a cold bath filled with tap-water. The thinking was about oxygenation, not metabolism. A fish just can't adjust that quickly. The chlorine in the tap-water couldn't have helped much, either.

The diary reminds me that it took two days to drain the pond. What it doesn't say is that, at first, I tried to do it by the siphon method and that is a blank in history because I was too ashamed to write it down. In order to get the siphon going, I used a vacuum cleaner for the first big suck. The vacuum cleaner hit back with a sizzle of a shock. Water had got in because I hadn't disconnected in time. Serves me right.

Discarding the cleaner, I did what I should have done at the start – used a submersible fountain pump connected to a hosepipe. It laboured away day and night. I joined it, with a bucket, lifting cubic yards of evil silt and chucking it at the flower beds.

Sometimes I was able to net another fish. These were put in a bucket of water which had been standing in the sun. They died instantly as well, stabbed in the back by our Rhode Island Reds. Ever noticed that chickens are instinctive killers? If it moves, jab it. If you were to lie on the ground and wink at a brown hen, she'd have your eye out.

Fortunately I had no time for winking at baleful hens because fish were still going into containers. I see the diary points out one interesting fact: even when I got down to the last of the dead mud the little carp were still full of energy. They jumped in the heavy scum. They charged banks of mud or carved mole-runs through it in order to escape the net. And, once in tap-water, they survived.

Soon after the pond was full again and a new range of plants installed, things calmed down. The carp settled back in, so did the newts and the frogs. The heron banked steeply at tree-top height and came to check things over.

I wondered if he might spear a hen or two, just for practice, but when they trundled up he flew away.

CHAPTER ELEVEN

Seasonable selfishness

We all know men and boys who observe the tench-fishing ritual on the dawn of June 16th because it seems the right thing to do. And so it is. There lies hope for all traditional values. But the question is: what would they think of tench-fishing if they'd been doing it for weeks already? If fishing seasons were abolished, then one minute after midnight on June 15th would not be a magic moment and June 16th would become a very ordinary mark on the calendar.

When there were fewer anglers – or, at least, fewer anglers who could travel very far or very often – and many natural waters, it probably didn't matter at all when you fished, or where. No great harm could be done. Now that there are buzzing millions and each one can be on a distant river by breakfast-time, it matters a lot.

If you see stream or lake, together with fish, weed and bankside growth as a balanced and quite fragile system, then surely it must have a rest from interlopers like us. Neither trout-stream fish stocks nor trout-stream fishing could stand a constant parade of water-whippers all the year round. No coarse river could or should, either. Each fish would be hooked six or seven times instead of two or three and you would need a bulldozer just to deal with the litter.

Well, maybe it wouldn't be quite as bad as that if they abolished the fence months and gave total freedom to everyone, but we would certainly lose time for creosoting the shed or painting the windows.

It's not as if we were actually deprived, is it? Even with the present restrictions, intensive angling and modern knowledge have shown us people who can take tench in winter, and carp too. Nowadays you can, if you like, fish for rainbows at almost any time of the year in some landlocked waters. Other waters are thinking of going that way.

There are even put-and-take coarse fisheries which will charge you gamey prices to fish in May. Indeed, I have no doubt that, at any time of the year, coach parties are travelling about in a distracted manner in the hope that they may be unloaded upon some place where the sense of time has no meaning.

We've all heard the arguments, of course. About how fishing in spawning seasons is not necessarily a Bad Thing, either because the fish don't really mind or because we can't be sure we've got the spawning times exactly right anyway.

You get the feeling that these old rows, coupled with the pressures of the age of leisure, are going to achieve a breakthrough for us. Leading abolitionists are likely to be those who want to make more money from fees and day tickets, and those who don't like bits of paper with rules on – and like paying for them even less. That, if you think about it, is a strange combination for a sense of crusading purpose.

Other people's seasons merge too and the pressures are not just upon angling. Nobody would be very surprised these days if someone bowled a football at Headingly, or had a goalkeeper leg before. But do today's kids want to fight with conkers taken from pickle jar or deep freeze, just as the Horse Chestnut candles are showing? (Do today's kids still have conker battles anyway?)

Would we mind if the race to get the first grouse to London was run every month of the year? Probably not, since there wouldn't be enough people to grouse about it. Quite certain it is, though, that most of us would wince in August to hear somebody whistling "Hark the Herald Angels". On the other hand, it could be that everybody is so used to chasing the sun by aircraft, and filling his freezer with exotic out-of-season foods, that the appropriateness of things has no meaning any more.

This Easter has been the warmest and mellowest in living memory – or, at least, in my memory. And now the dandelion seeds are flowing on the wind like the biggest hatch of fly ever seen. Sometimes the fish seem to be rising to the seeds, which cover the water and confuse the angler as well. Not many fish have been taken, but just to be out with the slender rod and shoulder bag is good enough.

From the old humped bridge we watched a man hook a pound brownie in the region of his waders as he stood a yard or so from the bank. Unseasonably enough, we were talking about barbel – perhaps that was because the stock trout below was caught on a worm. No we didn't shudder and snort – it's a liberal kind of syndicate which has the fishing.

In any case, people don't fish for barbel with worms any more, do they? It's a kind of folk memory from the days when barbel were unusual fish. Now every river worth the name seems to have them and almost every angler seems to have them out.

We didn't talk too much about old pouty-face, because we were holding trout rods, after all – and it was May. Anyway, I think we recognised a great truth.

The trouble with great truths is that everyone thinks they are very ordinary truths, once they're noticed. But part of this one is that a lot of anglers reckon there's an absolute need to let the seasons pass, and the fish with them.

One of the sensible developments in our time is that we have produced the general angler. Trout, salmon or coarse rod, fly, maggot, worm or luncheon meat; spinner or bread-flake . . . it's all the same because it adds up to year-long fishing. So what's the point in grasping at more than that?

For some reason, salmon men occasionally hook record barbel, the kind of fish which had been snapping swim-feeder traces only days before. With no coarse season to worry about such a fish might be listed for stardom. Now *that* would be a fine test of liberal progressive thinking.

Yes, obviously, the other bit of the great truth is that total freedom is no damn use at all.

There's a lake in our club waters book which is always closed until August 1st. All through June and July you can hear us saying to each other things like: "Know where you're going to be on August 1st."

Now it so happens that the lake is well worth waiting for since it's big, beautiful and bountiful, but that's only part of the point. The other part is that it is made even better through the build-up of expectancy. While I suspect most of us realise that there's value in waiting, we couldn't find that value at all unless we were made to wait. Anglers need the close season far more than the fish do. Giving them a breather may be good sense and charitable with it, but giving us one is the biggest boost we can give to our own enjoyment.

The close season is not a restriction at all – it is an excuse for selfishness.

CHAPTER TWELVE

Right against the evidence

I caught an eight-ounce roach back in the summer when my favourite swim was running a bit low. At another place, but in the same week, I struck the point off a fly called The Guv'nor which came to me in a rusty old tobacco tin and must have been the last of the line because nobody's heard of such a name these days. The trout who did the job must have weighed half a pound, like the roach. He was swimming in a favourite spot too, but it's the roach I remember.

Despite what the angling journalists are saying (ROACH COME BOUNCING BACK or BOOMTIME ROACH BONANZA) it all seems to be happening somewhere else. Roach are still the fish to talk about. Their disappearance was an event which made youth seem as far away as, in fact, it was. It was a slow nationwide decline rather than a sudden departure. We've had the odd big roach, but rarely several and never a bag, not even in our favourite swims.

Even with this situation depressing everybody, a once extremely well-roached river should grant a decent scattering of roach in a favourite swim, shouldn't it? Well, of course it should.

Let's dispose of the idea that I may have forgotten how to catch them – because once, not a hundred years ago, I was able to wander up to someone and talk about my four roach going on 1 ½ lb. Whereupon we both gazed at the sky to hear the bells of heaven ringing.

That was in my favourite swim and such a place should live up to its reputation, even in a roach famine. If it doesn't, then it gets demoted and becomes just any old stretch of water.

I wouldn't think about demoting this swim merely for its failure to make headlines with roach; it's purely a matter of being sensible. In fact, I'm going through a period of reform – the time has come to assess comparability studies, unit costs, productivity ratings and the market economy.

Quite simply, this favourite swim hasn't been delivering. It hasn't been worth the price of maggots. What's more, a check on the records shows that this has been the case for years – all species considered. So why have I been fishing it for so long, let alone calling it special? Perceptive point that – often wondered about it myself. Perhaps it's due to geography: the swim is only down the hill and round the corner from where I live. Or because I approach it through patches of sunlight in old woodland while the rest of the river bank is as bare as the second half of the twentieth century.

The place is an opening in a belt of trees and bushes. There's room for only one fishable spot, above or below, for a satisfactory number of yards. To get there you must leave the twisting path, duck under heavy cascades of berries from the Wayfaring Tree in autumn and be flayed by shoulder-high nettles. It is the way of the sentimentalist.

Once there, you can sit on your basket backed by two oak trees. Their branches lean over the water but at a considerate height. Even a lofty upward strike with a 13-foot rod will not quite reach them.

There's danger of getting tackle caught downstream though. The woodland strip sends feelers out over the water for some distance. But the curve of the bank and the push of the current gives a near-perfect long trot and there's no real need to send the float down too close, unless you believe that an old chub has tucked himself into the jungle.

In the woodland swim everything feels right. Forget what I said before about the cull per annum and the evidence of the record. Just writing about it has made all those harsh resolutions wear off. It looks right and it feels right.

A balsa Avon float with a long cane rudder, balanced, sunk and steadied by three or four AA shot will carve a magic path for you here. The killing run passes streamer weed over a hard bottom. I know exactly where the gravel bed dips and where it rises, where the current changes direction and where half a wagon wheel is buried with some of my leger weights attached.

I also know where the wrens come from and Master Robin o' the gentle tin. There's a kingfisher slash of blinding blue – or green, depending on the light – at least twice a day. And when the March wind blows, this is the last place it finds.

And you ask me about the fish? Well, so you should, I suppose. But shall we really bother with the facts about a favourite swim? As a general rule it's not very sensible to throw one's weights around since that can diminish the day and falsify the record. After all, three gudgeon, a salmon parr and forty-four minnows may be all it was possible to get on a particular afternoon and may stand quite well beside the returns elsewhere on the river.

Yes, there have been sessions at the woodland swim which added up like that. But don't forget those roach I mentioned. And there were three chub with them – clodhoppers all, and bolshie with it. And five dace to half-a-pound, together with a surprise perch of three-quarters-of-a-pound taken on bread-flake. Then there were two trout, 3 lb and 2 lb (returned) as well as gudgeon, salmon parr and minnows.

All that may not have happened so very long ago but I admit it was before metrication. This makes no difference, since anyone who mentions kilos by an English river deserves to be sent on a permanent package holiday to places where they eat everything they catch.

The angle on all this is pretty clear, though. While that particular day's fishing may have established the woodland swim as my favourite one, such a bag wasn't repeated. The trouble is that I keep thinking it's going to happen again.

Since that day I have usually managed to get a chub there and some dace, though not many of those. There have been grayling, one of them quite a thumper and I thought about ringing someone, sending off for accurate scales and searching for witnesses – that sort of thing. But I didn't.

Recently, running through the swim with casters, I missed about fifty bites. No, it wasn't all those minnows. This sort of thing often happens to me with casters anyway. I latched on to only two dace and was in communication, for just a second, with a heavy something that bored away low down and made me feel inferior.

But most of the time results have been below average to ordinary, or blanks. This is not the sort of treatment you expect from a favourite swim, particularly as I've had better fish – other than roach – elsewhere. So I decided to give it a rest and try others in line for the premier position.

You can't do that on trout waters of course, because you need much more space to work in. Yet I must say that there's a narrow-waisted spot where the current comes through compressed and gurgling, pushed there from the broad flat below the weir. It swirls under tree roots, gives a smooth polish to a gravel bar and then spreads itself out again a few yards below.

Here, I think, is a favourite spot. At least it's the one I first think of when getting the rod out of the car. The sort of place you keep in mind as you walk up, missing one fish here, another there. It's the vision for after sandwiches, or the last resort if the day really has gone badly.

The hole under the roots does hold good trout. You can see them. You can never see the grayling, though. A fancy fly will bring them up and down, attracting a pointed nose, a plunge and a tug before the splash has faded from the surface.

One such grayling hit the bright little Terry's Terror and immediately turned into a pound-and-a-half brownie. It's surprises like that which put a gloss on fishing moments and build the tradition of favouritism.

Trouting can never give you a deep sense of commitment to a particular place. I know that if nothing moves here I can walk on above the tail and wade the flat, casting up to the gushing gates. Cold pressure on the knees; warm hope above. Casting a hundred times with something always beckoning ahead, or to the side, or round the next curve of the stream – it's a fanciful, feckless business.

Passing the woodland swim on the bottom-fishing river, where life is steadier, homelier but somehow more complicated, I thought I'd just look in on it for old time's sake. Through the trees and over their leaves, hack through the nettles and make for the twin oaks.

A voice said: "Morning". I felt like a householder who has just heard a noise downstairs. A man was fishing my swim with his back to the oaks and his keepnet pegged in where mine had been since the days of the roach.

"Much happening?" I asked, mentally putting away the poker.

"Not a lot", he replied.

I told him I thought it was a nice spot anyway. He told me he'd been hearing about a chap who once caught four roach nearly 2 lb apiece from this swim.

"Oh yes", I said.

The kingfisher came by on his way to the sound barrier and the man said ''Best place on the river – I come here all the time.''

Not tomorrow, he won't.

CHAPTER THIRTEEN

Snoring in Sabland

When did you last see a sleeper by the river? Rod idle on the hot grass, maggots stinking, wellington boots coagulating in the sun? The question does not refer to Radio One picnickers or the sort of anglers who do it in white tee-shirts, since they don't count at all – except in the way a man reckons up life's irritations.

Perhaps this applied to me at one time, though it is many years since I was able to squeeze into a tee-shirt of any colour. Come to think of it, they weren't invented then anyway, at least not with slogans printed on them.

I saw a delicately-rounded girl in a bikini on the opposite bank last summer and the sight caused me to flip a Devon across without proper concentration and to wind-in so carelessly that any slumbering salmon would not have found it at all titillating. But the girl wasn't an angler. She was resting awhile after helping the other syndicate's keeper to trim the vegetation on that beat with a billhook and rake. He was obviously the husband or boy friend and emerged in a husky fashion within minutes. I think he was wearing a tee-shirt and he didn't deserve her. On our side of the water we don't seem to have assistants in bikinis. We don't have many salmon either, but at least we dress properly.

If angling is a sport then nobody will think of sleeping. If it is a pastime then striped deckchairs and an hour's zizz might be perfectly understandable. That's how cartoonists see us – comic characters in tramp's clothing snoring away with the line tied to a big toe, and all the fish popping out of the water and grinning.

Nowadays you never see a tramp, and most of the comics seem to be about war or discotheques or motor bikes, but we still don't know if fishing is something to snooze over. Personally, I think it is a mixture of sport and pastime, whipped together with bits of escapism all clouded by obsession. Which must mean that you don't go to sleep, because something might happen, even if it is only a cow treading on your rod.

Of course, if you sleep these days it may not be a cow but a Hunt Saboteur who breaks your rod. We've all been warned about the "sabs" (which is the shorthand term used by members of the British Field Sports Society) through the angling press and club newsletters. Lawyers have been employed to contribute advice in four paragraphs with only three sub-clauses. They contain words like: "If you have any advance warning of disruption, notify the police and request their attendance to prevent a breach of the peace." Great efforts are being made at this very moment to ensure that tee-shirted anglers from the hard cities do not defend the contemplative man's recreation by sweeping committed sabs into the water with mighty blows from brawny tattoo'd forearms.

Field Sportsmen have never been known to sleep on the job. Nobody has ever fallen off a horse because he had ridden into dreamland. A man doesn't snore with his 12-bore. Yet many of those who take their pleasures from the countryside believe that anglers *are* half-asleep and that they'd better wake up pretty quickly. They mean that we'll only bring the sabs down if we stick together and hunt 'em in a pack.

It so happens that a lot of anglers don't think they are anything to do with field sports. While that seems like dinosaur thinking, it does tie in with the problem of what angling really is. Somehow we cling to the idea that it has to do with natural man on his own natural earth, something individual, God-given, innocuous – rather like breathing, or thinking of pretty girls. But not sleeping, of course.

Despite being extremely clubbable and given to spending fishing days in long lines under green umbrellas, we do it only to gain personal happiness. The swim is ours for the day and no-one else's, bought for the price of a ticket or an annual payment to the club treasury. And the idea of having to do something energetic, like arguing about the politics of conservation or fighting for the right to cast a line on the river, is a bit alien, jarring and baffling.

But out in Sabland where the girls don't wear bikinis but flak-jackets, their sport is the pursuit of sportsmen. They hunt with vigour and make sure it all gets written up in the newspapers. End-of-day bag: four couple of lost hounds, one frothing Master, a colonel's coronary and two hunt followers charged with assault.

It hasn't happened to anglers yet, as far as I'm aware, and it probably never will. But while some sabs may be part of the cells of revolution the rest are thinly spread silly young malcontents; mere midges. One day we shall be able to buy a cream to spread on our arms and legs to keep away the sabs. In the meantime, though, it might be sensible to give the BFSS a friendly nod at least, if only because there are perils greater than sabbery. Brothers of the angle haven't been so very successful at keeping the rivers bright and brimming, so we'd better expand the family and all be brothers of the countryside.

Nothing is more likely to prevent a good night's sleep than the thought that the river may not be there in the morning. That nightmare is about the only thing I know which can take your mind off fishing pleasure, apart from a wisp of bikini.

I have fished opposite car-breakers' yards to the sound of thumping and screeching metal. I have fished above great machines scooping away the curves from river banks. I have fished dead streams below trout farms and retreated from the effluent haze. And I have seen the bed and bones of a river which had never shown them before in centuries of hot summers. Nobody in past days had felt the need to suck the water away or hurry it on to the sea so quickly, while moaning about the drought. Yes, it would be nice to close your eyes and have all that go away.

All that said, there's still a fair opportunity for the dreamless, blameless, innocent siesta of the solitary trout fisher away across the meadows and far from whistle and scales, towpath joggers or sab active-service units. There comes that sudden pause and dead time on even the best of bright waters when the last plop and fishy ring was an hour ago and the sun is beating down on your head and casting arm. The speeding chalk flow looks like tarnished chrome on such a hotplate day. Nothing moves. Nothing will move. Might as well expect a rise on the sands of Mars.

It is then that the baking boots must come off and the bag be taken from the shoulder. Not that I actually slept on that afternoon but I relaxed with my elbows on the grass and with my bared feet in the sacred water. Yet I swear that I tied no line to my big toe.

Strangely, the sun seemed to have moved down quite a bit when the first plop was heard downstream, and I'd been listening hard for it all the time. Then there was another one upstream. Not coots or voles, not this time. The upstream commotion was coming quite regularly. Time for action again.

I grabbed the rod, shouldered the bag and did a fast crawl up to the bend above me. There he was, lifting and lipping at iron blues coming down in line astern. Six feet out, I estimated, on station and packing in the snack.

The cast had to be made in a round-arm fashion both to avoid a bush which seemed to have crept up behind me and to negotiate the tussocky promontory which formed the bend of the bank. Detaching the fly from the keeper ring where it had been idling during the rest period, I noticed that it was a Gold-Ribbed Hare's Ear. In my box were some Houghton Rubies. I didn't make the change, though it might have been better to have done so. The old excitement, I suppose.

On one knee now, I worked out some line, thinking . . . wrong fly but right size . . . mind the bush . . . don't bungle it. I bungled it. Again, excitement.

Fortunately, a trout just upstream, rising six feet from the bank, does give you a fair chance to come in at him from the side without laying your leader over his head. But you must still be a cool caster. So I got a mental grip on things and waited.

The fly had landed in a loop of nylon and the line tip had smacked the water. Had I put him down or, more likely, sent him powering back to the streamer weed for a quick check on things?

Plop. There he was again, bless him, back on station. He took with a kind of sideways sip, turn and dive, rather like a grayling, but he was a nice brownie. The rod shuddered as he did a fast zigzag almost to the width of the river and back again. The cane bent, nodded and hardened against him. I stripped in some loose line by hand and was forced to let it out again. Then he was in the net and on the bank with the priest tapping him.

"That's a good fish", said a voice behind me. For a very small second I thought it might be a sab creeping up on me and I wondered if priests were good for them too, but sabs don't admire trout in cultured accents. This could only be the owner of the fishing. My host for the day in fact, though my presence had been arranged through a friend. What was that he was carrying in his hand? My green wellies, of course. And what was I doing? Standing in bare feet, of course.

Well, worse things have been known to happen in this world, and bare-footedness is no crime. But somehow you feel defenceless and vaguely guilty about taking a trout like that. A girl may approach the river wearing two slight strips of cotton: a matchman may signal his presence in the greenery by wearing a white tee-shirt. But a portly trout fisher, invited to holy places, is not expected to act like a pilgrim on his knees unshod.

All I said was: "Yes, a nice fish", and thanked him for the day. He didn't look at my feet, just put the boots down neatly, brushed his hands together and hoped that I would get another decent trout.

A sab would have chucked the boots into the middle of the river.

CHAPTER FOURTEEN

A bid for Bumblies

There was this auction the other week and it did things for me.

Thing no. 1 was . . . even in a long hot summer with the upper Avon trout frying themselves lethargically in a molten flow under spreading duckweed I could feel sympathy for blokes who don't know about built cane.

Thing no. 2 was . . . even with smaller streams disappearing in the odd hiss of steam, or down the occasional illicit garden hosepipe, I had the opportunity to make a big discovery about artificial flies.

The blokes who turned up at the auction weren't really blokes – they were chaps. In violent sports jackets, tweedy hats and with an air of authority. Six of them there were, so far as I could see, all eager. In the corner of the sale-room, behind a Chippendale-style thingummy, three broken brollies, something catalogues always call a jardiniere, and a barometer, was the reason for their eagerness.

Eight fly rods in bags, together with some large cardboard boxes. In those boxes were more trout flies than a man can look upon without becoming as baffled as a chameleon in an over-heated maggot factory.

The chaps were there for the rods. So was I – but I'd been on the viewing day before, when I'd had a chance to look at them. The chaps hadn't bothered to look, beyond taking a quick squint before the auctioneer came in.

Now if you're buying old cane – indeed, any cane – you just can't make do with a quick squint and rely upon a catalogue saying "Hardy". That was the trouble, of course. They were ancient cane, by Hardy and Farlow and similar fine names from the days of style and empire. In other words, the stuff of which snap judgements are made.

In case nobody's realised it, such rods are now sought-after much as you might seek any other old and rare work of art. They aren't just nice fishing rods any more. That's why the bidding put the chaps on their mettle. I watched one of them mystify the auctioneer (a wise and experienced man) so much that he actually blinked behind his hammer as the bidding mounted for a bit of wood. Pounds went skittering about like a hatch of Mays in the past when the rods were active.

I had seen the faults in those rods – the raddled seams and painful splicing, their aching spines and those nasty hairlines opening and shutting above the ferrules. At best, 20 years of misuse; but mostly 50 years of sabre-rattling.

OK, so I felt like warning the nearest bidder when he was hovering around £40 for an 8½-footer which had such a fiendish set in its tip that it wasn't worth trying to put the thing back in the bag. But you don't warn bidders at auctions; your motives are likely to get bashed about a bit. He paid £42 in the end and looked pleased, so maybe he knew something I didn't. I just reckoned that the trout were safe.

The big value for me in all this, was that by the time the eight rods had gone, the chaps' wallets had thinned a lot. So when we got to the flies and other bits and pieces, I was in with a good chance.

There was only a little in-fighting to do in advance. A few Pall Mall-ish and St James's empty fly boxes, with windows, catches and compartments, reached the prices they deserved and went to those who pretend to know nothing about the virtues of sticky-back foam in tobacco tins.

Then I missed a rather nice reel, got beaten to the rise on a trout bag and landed two big boxes packed with flies, wet and dry, unused, unrusted, tied by Master Twinklefingers himself and packed up by somebody who shouldn't have. It was like opening cartons of dense wool.

For £6 I now have enough flies to last a lifetime, should I be so lucky as to have a lifetime. And if I'm not so lucky then my beneficiaries will be able to turn an honest profit by stocking all the tackle shops in the south of England.

After several evenings with classification lists, tweezers and a magnifying glass, I still sat between mounds of unsorted flies and saw myself growing arthritic before identifying the last handful.

Then I made the great mental leap forward. It was a discovery which may have been made before me, but only by men who kept very quiet about it. In the face of every artificial known to fly-tyers, from Dave Collyer back to grunting inventors with blackthorn hooks and goat hair, I realised that I didn't know enough to describe them all. Grinding to a halt between 21 Grannoms and 8 Treacle Parkins, I ran out of names. After the panic, I acted in self-defence.

Now hear this: all flies, whatever, their colour, shape, size or form, can be fitted into the following basic classifications:

Dry	Wet
Smuttygnatties	Nymphs
High Whiskies	Fryflies
Palmers	Flashers
Spents and Sparse	
Exotics and Bumblies	

If anyone doesn't think much of all this, then bad cess to him. All I can say is that he'll never have such simple fishing as I now enjoy.

The genus High Whiskies, for instance, would give confidence to anybody faced with something strange that floats well and delicately. My system means that there's always somewhere to put something, without going to evening classes first, or feeling inferior. Leave it to the chaps to waste time pondering the merits of this or that while the fish are moving. If it's small specks that the two-pounders are mopping up, then no messing – go straight to the Smuttygnatties and pick anything that looks right.

No need to worry, now, if your favourite supplier slips up on a BWO, say, and produces a monumental thorax in thick brown and gold. All you have to do is demote this mystery creation from the High Whiskies section and place it happily among the Exotics and Bumblies.

CHAPTER FIFTEEN

Painful problem

When my dentist started telling me how he used a Grey Wulff at mayfly time, I raised my eyebrows; not in surprise, nor even in disapproval, but because that's all I could do. He had stuck that curved gurgling and sucking thing into my mouth.

Privately, I doubted if the fish were quite ready for mayfly on his part of the Test, since mayfly have a habit of coming up in June. I tried to indicate something of this with eyebrow language, grunts, snorts and two-fingered actions (meant to imitate happy mayflies). But you know how it is in The Chair.

"Yes", he said, "late May and June", and chatted happily on. Skilful translators, dentists, and well practised at the monologue. He was on to Spring Olives when the drill began its mosquito whine, and that's not an insect that gives you memories of gentle days.

Once it was fashionable for dentists to have fish tanks in front of The Chair. You could peer over the glass of pink water, stare round the rack of unmentionables which nobody gets curious about, and see goldfish or angel-fish swimming around. The theory was that this had a calming effect.

My dentist got rid of the tanks one day – I think because he needed the space for more tools. Now he has a picture of the Test Valley on the wall and talks about fishing instead. This is effective. At least it works as well as anything can when you have a mouthful of steel . . . so long as you don't get to pondering that old, useless question about how the fish feels without benefit of anaesthetic.

Some people think that fish don't feel pain at all, and can prove it. Well, almost. Others think that they do and can prove that, more or less. Most people hear the fine arguments and decide to stay agnostic because life's easier that way.

I had a long talk with a famous novelist in Devon who said that he'd had a long talk with Thomas Hardy in distant days. Hardy had said that he reckoned trees could feel pain. I refuse to make the obvious remarks about bright young willows giving us reproachful glances as we break off bits to release flies, floats or leger weights. After all, it may be true but we prefer not to notice.

My arguments about fish and pain always come down to blood and philosophy. While humans die under torture or in warfare, some of us think it is a mere affectation to agonise over the top lip of a dace. Which doesn't mean that you shouldn't care, just that you shouldn't howl.

Having seen the ripping motion and sideswipe on the gunwhale, mast or decking practised as a ritual by certain boat-fishing sea anglers when the mackerel or dogfish are about, I reckon that my trout are killed with a certain amount of care and dignity.

As for commercial trawling procedures – there's really nothing to be said which hasn't been said before. Still, if you really want to open it up again, then let the vegetarians in on the debate. Light them carefully and then retire to a safe distance; and if you can find an "Animal Aider" or a "League Against Cruel Sports" representative as well, then you'd do better to make the safe distance somewhere on the far horizon.

A kindly club member with some giddy connections in the Test Valley gave me a day with him. It wasn't all that far from my dentist's fishing grounds but I didn't think to mention, while in The Chair, that I had a decent sort of time with the macaroni. Yes, of course I was after grayling and, no, I'm not a grocer. It just happens to be a fact that macaroni is good for grayling, but that's just by the way and I'd just as soon avoid telling everyone about it.

I settled down below a bend with the frost hard about me and brightness in the sky. The swim was a run pushing out from the crisp curve of the bank and settling in a turbulent race three-quarters of the way across the river. Depth: eighteen inches to two feet. Against this combination I put up a cane rod for old time's sake and a closed-face reel for efficiency's sake. A small balsa float sat on a single swanshot and the 3 lb line ran through to a no. 10 hook.

In these boily, shallow swims it always seems best to let the bait trundle where it will, with no shot on the cast length, so long as the line between float and rod tip is encouraged to behave in a disciplined manner.

What superb fish were those grayling. Tiny indications on the float and a shooting, corkscrewing, boring weight on the wrist. The strike socked home, meeting hard fish in hard frost on a song of a day. Among them was a trout or two, of course, and this is the point – there was a particular trout with a white patch behind his pectorals. After I'd shaken this trout off the hook in the water, he struck again within the next cast or two. Gently unhooked again. Pause. Catch a grayling. Run down again – thump. The same trout.

My companion left his swim and came up to watch. I tell you I hooked that trout six times. In the end I moved to another place because he was making me nervous.

Whatever you want to say about this trout's persistence, you could also say about his idiocy. We worry about pricking a fish on the fly. We creep and crawl and ring changes right through the box because we think that a particular trout has been alarmed by our previous offering, or has become suspicious of it as an item of food.

Yet here I was, sinking a hefty no. 10 into him six times and he would still have come back for more. Macaroni is good, but it's not magical stuff. It has no pain-killing properties, as far as I know. Incidentally, maybe the groundbaiting effect of two or three small pieces thrown in from time to time made the incident of small value as a guide to fly fishing. After all, you can't groundbait with flies. On the other hand isn't nature supposed to be doing that for us? What's a hatch or a fall of spinners if not surface-baiting at least?

Well I don't say that any of this proves much at all, but since other people have had similar experiences it does make you think. Anyway, for those who like to feel the strength of their consciences occasionally, it seems fair to say that killing fish is probably worse than hooking them. Not a matter of pain, but of removing a fellow creature from the world.

Of course, the trout or the salmon or the grayling doesn't know he is being taken from a place of dash, splash and beauty to a place of blackness. That kind of thinking is only for people who polish up their guilt for the fun of it. Yet we know what happens, don't we? It's to do with our view of the world. The connection between us and the friend on the end of the thrumming monofil is severed by the bang on the head.

My way out of this disloyal taking of friends is to make a kind of libation to the river gods. The rule is fixed and firm. When I've caught the first trout of the day, he is returned to his element. No argument. Whatever his size, he is allowed to slide away after unhooking. I salute him and wish him well. Mind you, if this sounds like I'm moving close to holiness (or, at least, nature worship, which may be the same thing) then let me say that I always hope that the first fish of the day will be undersized.

After that little ceremony I'll bop a brace with the feeling that they are well deserved, even if it hurts me more than it hurts them. And if the only fish I catch is right at the end of the day, and he weights 2 lb, what then? Next question, please.

I was preparing to raise some of this hypocritical nonsense with the dentist, once he'd finished with the drill, but we got on to fluoride in the drinking water, which rather gets me going. So I never did.

In six months' time we might, perhaps, discuss these weighty matters. Well perhaps not. He might laugh so that his hand shakes – and I'm a bit of a coward when it comes to pain.

CHAPTER SIXTEEN

What to grab when you run

Reading will not necesarily make you a better angler. It may make you a very great thinker and enable you to beat better anglers round the head with your knowledge . . . but a fish doesn't care if he has a bookworm on the other end of the rod. It's the worm on the hook that counts.

If you want to measure it by results, then fishing must be a practical business for practical men. But we can't all be taught, personally and by example, at the side of the great rodbenders. And however great some of them may be, if they just let out the odd grunt in your direction you'll not only be baffled, you'll feel let down.

Be it known, though, that after a lot of reading and collecting of fishing books I can point to the occasional little success which was due to turning a page rather than leaning on luck or instinct. And sometimes they've kept me going in happy hopefulness over a dismal run of bad days.

There's something sensual about fishing books of all kinds, whether well-written, badly written, old, new-born, to be remembered or fashioned entirely as jumble-sale supplies. Mind you, I can't say that I've ever found a decent fishing book in a jumble sale. In dealers' back rooms, cold and silent, yes – but not in the church hall. Perhaps the vicar pinches them first.

Some back rooms in second-hand bookshops have a kind of religious feeling about them, if only that of the crypt or the family vault. Here the long-dead sleep like brown and crinkled leaves locked into an ice-bound river. But not to worry: booksellers have woken them all up by putting on 21st-century price tags.

Now ancient colonels are stirring again and dreaming of reincarnation in paperback. Craggy ghillies cunningly knuckle their forelocks once more, muttering monosyllabic witticisms which once had forgotten house-party guests choking in polite gurgles of amusement.

If you happened to be "back from France" in time for the last trout season, wrote John Waller Hills. Doesn't that say so much? How many of us didn't come back from France, or now can only do so on the car ferry. What was the trout season like in 1919 or any other year around the time of *A Summer on the Test*?

Despite my traditional and expected affection for Harry Plunket Greene's *Where the Bright Waters Meet* (which cost my wife credit card money when she bought me a first edition), Hills' book is the finest I know on chalk-stream trouting.

Not long ago, in a trout season far closer to Cruise missiles than whiz-bangs, I took Waller Hills' practical, precise and thoughtful prose to the river and read it among the kingcups while waiting for the first rise upstream. It didn't work. Serves me right, grabbing at mixed pleasure in that manner. Even the shining water, all unmarked by rings, was superior to JWH's pull. The mind was flummoxed. So Hills and I ended up in No Man's Land. Even angling books should not be brought too close to their subject.

The nice thing about collecting fishing books is that you can afford to be dogmatic about them – which, of course, you shouldn't be about anything that happens at the waterside.

We heard at the end of the last coarse season that the biggest perch was caught by the friend of a member. It was over 2½ lb and taken on bread-crust casually dropped in for a couple of hours. "What's this?" he said. Ah, well . . . no book ever written has recommended crust for perch . . . not even in the great days of style and poetry.

Another nice thing is that you don't have to go back to Arthur Ransome or Waller Hills to find the first and the last of the best. Some – very few I grant, but some – are writing the best now. That's really something, because these are not the best times for the job.

If I had to make a list of the top fishing books, judged on style and significance (one without the other is like fishing with beautifully arranged tackle and no hook) then Brian Clarke's *The Pursuit of Stillwater Trout* would be in there and glowing bright. So, surely, would his work with John Goddard – *The Trout and the Fly* – which has advanced our awareness of what the fish sees, and in which words and photography blend so happily.

For coarse fishing (I prefer the term "bottom fishing" but I don't want to sound old-fashioned) the best service has certainly come since the last war.

Those who went fishing by the first bus and soaked hooks to gut before walking two miles to catch that bus, still remember what a sudden, dramatic thing was Richard Walker's *Still Water Angling*. It is now recognised as one of the great works and so needs no special mention from some bloke dusting off his books in 1986. But Walker didn't stop there.

As I've said before, Walker's writing is literature and his books are underrated if people think of them merely as holding their places by advancing knowledge. Of course, he's done that, but he also gave a nudge to the way angling is written about. Take it from me, we might still be making do with those dubious old ghillies if Walker hadn't looked up from his lawnmower.

He seems to have done a bit towards establishing the cult of personality in coarse fishing at a time when being a personality didn't mean that you had to win the world angling championship at the end of a long glass-fibre pole. He promoted a group of friends and acquaintances, who then went forth to spread the word as individuals, becoming household names in the process. This cosy group of literate and thinking anglers was operating at just the right time. There was a gap in the chummery of coarse-fishers, and they filled it with information. They became the people everybody wanted to fish with – and their books made that possible.

Naturally, things began to change as anglers became more sophisticated, began to read more and travelled by car rather than bus or train. Then the cult of personality became merely a system for setting up whipping boys. Jack had become as good as Richard and the writing of the Grand Master himself, as well as of his acolytes, began to look a mite insular.

And now, years later, loyal fans like me begin to notice the stories coming back in new guises, as old discoveries are dressed up for modern times. This is not a gibe at those who built the past for me, since home truths are no less true for being the same as before, and there really is nothing so very new that it is clearly a revelation.

One man who put a rod in the hands of the most interesting people (which means those who were boys when I was a boy) was Bernard Venables. He is properly honoured on my shelves as the writer who indeed taught in prose-poetry. He's the chap who got you to save your pocket money after just five minutes with *Mr Crabtree Goes Fishing*. This was a picture book with floats you could feel, reels you could covet and a total angling atmosphere you could smell, taste and revel in. Later, when you had more money, you read his elegant *A Fisherman's Testament*, his books on the history of the sport, his guide to angling waters . . . in fact, everything he wrote.

There has been no more evocative stuff than this. He distilled the essence and, I truly think, said it all – or all that was worthwhile. After a time you found yourself wondering why anybody else should bother to produce descriptive writing – or drawing, come to that. Venables had surely cornered the market for all time.

Sadly, though, the seeds of decay were in it. No, not decay, but satiety. His work was like Christmas cake – it was giddy richness. Too finely mixed to give you indigestion, but enough to make you pine for bread and water. This was not a fault in him, but in his readers who gorged themselves.

Some of the most satisfying books are now lost even to those who play the game of thinking what they should grab when fleeing from a fire.

I'm remembering Geoffrey Bucknall's little *Fishing Days* – a modest offering about boyhood years and onward. Pull that one out and it can put a smile on the faces of those who have grown fat in size and experience. Small fry like that, long eclipsed by their authors' greater and later efforts, still have staying power. Like Maurice Wiggin's *The Passionate Angler* and BB's much loved *Confessions*. He's always forgiven for telling us to use alasticum wire for carp fishing (saying it would cut through lily stems), because he chatted to us in the right way.

The older books made you *feel*. Modern ones are so confoundedly useful. One of those who bridged this divide was Captain L. A. Parker. His *This Fishing* came like a gunshot. Perhaps they didn't think so at the time (just after the war), because this one wasn't just thin and modest: it was positively home-brewed and homespun. Only recently, so it seems to me, have we seen that book as being among the first of the 'No Messing – Now Hear This If You Want Fish' kind of writing. The first and the best. But Parker could afford to be brisk and commanding because he did have some new ideas. He also had the credentials (149 roach over 2 lb, for a start!).

There are wrinkles even in his footnotes. He demands that you use four loaves of bread for groundbait if you want to catch 2 lb roach: "I've taken at least eight loaves with me for one day's fishing when the water has been fast", he says. Then there's an asterisk and down below is the line: "Written before bread rationing, of course!" Even the exclamation mark is history.

As it happens, I often fish where Parker fished and know that there aren't many 2 lb roach left, even if I do throw eight loaves into the water. No, it's not just me. The cause is changing times – both in groundbaiting style and the quality of a river.

In case anybody is on the edge of believing that modern angling textbooks aren't doing their job, because of the power of nostalgia – well, I never said that. It is still true, nevertheless, that if you lump all the new items of learning together, you'll find they will quite easily fit into a bait tin. Maybe quite a large bait tin, but not big enough to wallow in.

That little dribble of cynicism doesn't matter a jot, though, when you have Billy Lane's *Encyclopedia of Float Fishing*. Ghosted by Colin Graham in a creative act, it saved me from a course of tranquillisers when I was having an updating session. Together with *Match Fishing to Win* (by the same team) this book represents all you need to know, while feeling modern. As with all the best instruction manuals, these have a touch of character to go with the talk of wagglers, duckers, onions, Trent Trotters and Sliding Antennas. Mr Lane and his friendly ghost also earned my gratitude for being the first to teach me how to tie an effective sliding stop-knot for stillwater sliding floats.

Going back a bit you can stumble on another landmark – Peter Stone's unpretentious *Legering*. It turned the twitch of the line over a finger into an art form. It taught us about sensitivity and the delicately poised rod tip when most people were sunk in "second rod" legering and leaving that to fish for itself.

Yet even Mr Stone was no prophet. He couldn't take us ahead just a few more years – paces almost – to the era of swing tips, quiver tips and swim feeders. Later he made up for it, but his chance of immortality had gone. But I suspect that didn't bother him at all, because he was just a bloke telling us what he'd found out . . . but telling us rather better than most. Because he *is* better than most. It's as simple as that.

Among the most recent writers, Peter Lapsley is doing fine work on small-lake trout fishing. And he's doing it in a way which encourages you to believe that all is well with angling books. Clear and crisp, without frills or dawdling, there are Walkeristic echoes which mark a noble line of descent. That is how it should be – the new building on the bricks of the old. It is possible to imagine Lapsley many years ago writing in ink to some learned journal of the art, while sitting in a country summerhouse.

Anybody who wants to take his fishing as he does his computer studies knows that there are many beautifully laid out, heavily pictured, clearly presented aids to the machinery of it all. What's that? You want soul as well? Well you might have to drift back among the oldies then, or be careful what you take from among the new men. You won't find any of it in the videotape libraries.

What about salmon anglers though? At one time all the books were about the King of Fish and written like that too. Well salmon men can read what they like, because it can't make much difference to that strange sport. For my money, they'd do well to stick with Colonel S. H. Crow's *Hampshire Avon Salmon.* He'd have got on well with Captain Parker, would Crow. It's a short, brisk book, as reliable as the military moustache.

While I don't think that deep study of salmon literature will take you all that much further than crossed fingers and a humble prayer, there is one book which all should read if they are to stay human and find in that irritating fish some sense of purpose. Henry Williamson's famous *Salar the Salmon* is not strictly an angling book, but it'll set you up to cope with a lifetime of blank days. Some of us think that Williamson, though an average sort of water-whipper, happens to be one of the greater writers of the age, so if anybody chooses to read his novels instead of other people's fishing books, then I shall quite understand.

So here they all are, then: names parading along the walls. From Cholmondeley-Pennell with tissue paper over his pike to the latest bright flood of colour printed in Italy or Czechoslovakia. There's Negley Farson's *Going Fishing* – nice enough but never quite earning its status as a classic. You can jump from Colin Willock to Ivan Marks, but that's a perilous way of staying in the swim.

Which ones would I rescue as the flames roar? Who's first for safety before the roof falls in? All of them of course. And if there's no time? If the roof's falling and I can only take one? Sorry, that's not a fair question and I wish I hadn't started this game. Frankly, if it came to that sort of crunch then armchair friends would have to fend for themselves – I'd just run. The important thing is to live to fish another day.

CHAPTER SEVENTEEN

Wonder what's in there?

The village school was digging out the village pond. Each child was of a size which shows precious little above a pair of wellington boots. There were about twenty of them and they didn't get wet.

They had worked out that the village pond, in the old days, was at the lowest point of a field near the green. So they got their little spades, and an enthusiastic teacher, and dug a hole there. Or rather, a number of holes which more or less linked up.

Some idlers suggested that the kids might do a better job if they got the local builder to come along with his excavating machine – but that wouldn't have been the same at all. Still, it would be a splendid thing to see the dampish patch at the corner of the meadow, beside the lane and to the left of the thatched cottages, turned into a pond again.

When the pixie workers had gone back to the classroom to learn about the ecology of ponds and so on, the excavation stayed as they had left it. After some months it still has no water in it. Either drainage systems have altered over the years or, more likely, the village pond was never there at all. Perhaps it's just as well that they didn't wake up next morning and find rippling water. While that might have earned them marks for achievement each one of them would have known that he or she had trodden all over it.

To a child, or an old man (or anyone) a village pond should be legendary and pleasantly mysterious. "I remember", says a wrinkled ancient, sitting under the old oak and staring at the water, "I remember when Mad Jack drowned in there."

"Don't forget your coats, children", says the teacher at the end of the day – adding, as a ritual, "And mind the pond as you go home."

But who could drown in a pond which you know for certain contains nothing interesting on the bottom at all, not even the bones of Mad Jack? What's more, a pond that can never even creep over the tops of your boots.

Perhaps this is why many of us aren't keen to go on grown-up expeditions called clearance parties. Most clubbable anglers are asked to go on clearance parties. Some are even ordered to the working group on pain of excommunication if they don't turn up.

The club newsletter gives you the time and place, with cheery promises of ten minute's labour cutting out fishable swims with logging saws, pulling on ropes attached to grapnels, . . . then away to the pub. In fact what happens is that the long, lean, wiry ones work away as if they were after subsidies from the Common Market. And rather older, heavier ones keep wondering about closing time. In the end, your captain's hand smites you on the shoulder and you feel like a good chap for having played the game – if rather sore.

In fact, something occurs which is far worse than that – and is the reason why, in addition to laziness, I don't always pull my weight on such outings. Put it this way: I don't want to see a bewitching lake with her knickers showing.

It's the village pond-maker's problem again. How many times have you gazed at a carrier stream running deep, or noticed the way a shelf on a bend falls away so you can no longer see gravel? Down there, everybody says,

is where the big ones are. Too deep a place for the great
sensuous billowing weed tresses to flourish. Or look at the
lake out of season: you peer through bankside bushes at
that black patch beyond the lily fringe. Shadowy, dark,
compelling . . . almost anything could happen if you try
there in June.

Along comes the weed clearance group with equipment
on their backs. Somebody in waders hardly breaks his stride
and walks straight in to the water. That mysterious,
fathomless spot barely comes up to his thighs!

Once I saw an energetic water-renovator walk up a
weir pool. And he wasn't wearing chest waders, either.
Until that moment it had always seemed to me to be quite
an impressive weir; now it looked small. The fierce current
had been made into a trickle.

Clearance parties dominate the thing they love, and
destroy with duty. They may be necessary, but they throw
away the sense of wonder, with the snags uprooted and
the caves under old tree-roots exposed as mere muddy
indentations in an ordinary bit of bank.

There aren't many places in Britain where an angler
can get a primitive shiver or two at the sheer power of his
medium. Few riverscapes exist in which you can see
yourself as a mere speck in the scene, pecking away at
mighty forces. Even if you think of legering under Niagara
Falls, say, you might look up and see someone coming
down on top of you in a barrel.

Yet it isn't so much size, or grandeur that
matters – just the thought that there is so much to discover.
If imagination can't work, then you are only half a
fisherman.

On our river we didn't know we had barbel. At times
we've wondered if anything swims in there at all, but let's
leave that idea for the moment. Barbel were the talking-
point at this moment, and our secretary called in a team
of heavies from London, Manchester and places like that.

They were barbel experts and they unpacked their specialist tackle like contract killers.

At the end of a day and a night they said they'd hooked barbel who did what they liked with them, as well as smaller ones who'd tried and failed. We were all pleased about this and looked at the home river as if we were seeing it for the first time in glorious sunlight. It was a big barbel river after all!.

Just to make sure, the secretary – who is a careful and dedicated man in a cynical sort of way – then called in the electro-fishers. With something like awe he reported that the barge had made only a thin sweep down one bank . . . but the fish, you should've seen them! The river's thick with barbel . . . four and six-pounders all over the place, eight and ten-pounders too. Name your weight: it's there. And all lying in the broad, fast straight below the weir.

At about this stage we were still happy merely to join in the rejoicing. It was, we thought, a legitimate discovery. Of course, it would have been a bit better to have found it out for ourselves by skilful angling, watercraft and natural observation – but there you are.

Once or twice I found myself talking in pubs with men who spent their weekends in wet suits with oxygen cylinders on their backs. One had built up a collection of Victorian bottles and even older stuff as a result of his trips along the river bed. Another had found a boat once, buried in gravel. But it was the third diver who worried me. "I know the bit of river you fish", he said.

Obviously he meant that he knew what my river looked like from underneath – he had penetrated the secret places. I should have finished my pint then. I should have said goodnight. I should have run away. But I didn't, of course.

"Been all the way up to your weir", he said. I was trapped by the fascination and asked him to describe it.

He told me it was clear down there and he could see everything. Once he'd grabbed the tail of an old pike, or very nearly. I wondered if he had got as close to the barbel.

"Barbel?" he asked.

"Yes, all those barbel in the straight below the weir."

"Nothing there at all", he said, "apart from the odd chub."

Then I saw my lovely river as indeed being as empty as the village pond that never was. If they weren't in the straight any more, then probably they were somewhere else – that must be it. And surely that means there's an undiscovered barbel swim for us to find again.

All the same, I didn't tell the others what he'd said.

CHAPTER EIGHTEEN

Pub crawl

Give me a moment and I'll talk about fishing inns. Or even fishing pubs. Or fishing Chinese takeaways. Trouble is, I can't think of one all that easily.

Yes it is possible to read of pubs – usually called "hostelries" and with 'Mine Hosts' – which seem to be what everyone is looking for. And you can talk to people who say that they put up at this splendid fishing inn with rod-racks all round the stables and maggots in the fridge. Somehow, though, you never remember the address they gave you.

You can read ads which say you're only a short walk from good fishing, or close to well-stocked lakes. Packed lunches are prepared for anglers, much as shovels might be cleaned for road-menders or boots polished for licentious soldiery. Most of these are places which may be quite as happy to take overflow conference delegates or travelling men who move from h. and c. and colour TV in all rooms, to the same amenities on the other side of Britain . . . without once looking over a bridge at a river.

Note that I do not say you can't find comfortable places, close to waterways, which don't mind having anglers paying the bill. You can, and we all have. But for those who see a fishing day as a well-rounded occasion, you need more than a base for operations.

You need what grandfather is said to have had. He alighted at some small railway halt to be assisted with his bags, rods, creel and net by a happy porter who had come up all red-cheeked and puffing after watering the roses. Remember happy porters? Oh come on, they lasted well beyond fob watches and half a sov. at Christmas.

A gentle cab ride from the station, down the lane by a clear stream, brought grandfather to his small anglers' rest. This had a pair of brassy scales in the summerhouse and a stuffed pike in the dark but welcoming hall.

At the bar were men with pipes who sat there, in the same seats, drinking from their own pewter tankards, for the same week at the same time every year. They were known by their nicknames as they toasted the 2 lb roach on the wall, which was always there every year, too, and had its own nickname.

The landlord would suggest that grandfather walked a bit of the river with him before dinner. And if it was a trouting place then your brace was served for breakfast – one for you and one for the landlord's family, as part of the tradition of the establishment.

Well, all right, perhaps we only *think* it might have been like that. Optimists, though, believe that the next time they head for new fishing grounds they will find the very place and a smiling publican with time to spare, so he can prove that in fishing the important things don't change.

In a decently bleak part of Scotland a few seasons back, when I was still an optimist, I stopped at a huge place by a loch. It had a sensible piece of split cane leaning against the wall outside. Here, I was sure, there would be found the company of robust salmon men behind the door.

Inside, it merely had corridors and empty rooms. I rang a handbell on a bamboo table and a lady in black took note of my need for a drink to drown disappointment.

The scotch came towards me on a tarnished silver tray borne by a tarnished retainer whose shuffling step echoed for five minutes before he reached me. He shook his head in a sort of peaty bafflement when I asked about the fishing. Then he disappeared into the gloom.

A little later, as I moved to a cold and peeling conservatory and sat on a bamboo chair, a passing hospitable highlander came out of a corridor. He said no, they didn't have any fishing. Where could I find some? He said most visitors asked at the Post Office. We looked out of the window at heather, loch and hillside. No Post Office. When I turned back to him, he'd gone.

No-one else hove in sight. There was just me and the bell and the bamboo furniture and the corridors. I wondered what I was doing there. So, obviously, did they. So I left. When I got outside I noticed that the cane rod had gone. Maybe someone from another corridor had taken it back to the Post Office.

Of course, you don't let this kind of thing bother you. It doesn't automatically follow that bleak hotels, or even inglenook-cheery hotels in the middle of good fishing country, don't care about the image of the sport which lives only in one's own mind.

Some places, a few, do deserve their situation. Like the big-value, low-cost, highly recommendable, find-of-a-pub in Yorkshire where my bedroom window opened on to a jovial little bit of rough trout stream containing few fish, and small ones, but miles of fascination.

At this pub the muddy boot is not noticed, the day-ticket book always handy and the bar always crowded. It isn't crowded with fishermen, though. Darts players, yes. Shepherds and horsemen, yes. Anglers, no. All that doesn't matter, because everything else is right and it's really asking too much for the last piece in the pattern. There is no local figure, who has fished there man and boy for fifty years. Nobody ever hands you a strange fly or fixes you with honest gaze and reveals secrets which will turn small trout into big ones.

Aeons ago in the south country I stayed at a pub by a weir where the sound of cold water bubbling put you to sleep and, in the morning, you were never out earlier than the landlord. He used a 14-foot steel rod, I remember, and ran an elder-pith float down the stream. It seemed to dip to a good roach on every cast. You could watch it happening as you shaved and after a remarkable breakfast (steak, I remember) he'd find time to go out again for an hour and show that he could still make it happen.

It was there that I saw my first otter, caught my first grayling and was broken by my first barbel. Yes, it was a long time ago – not quite as far back as grandfather's day, but near enough.

They knocked down that pub and demolished the old weir, replacing it at a lower level with a weir made of galvanised steel and neat, rectangular concrete. Then they turned the road into a motorway. That meant the anglers from London could get there much faster, but they had to find somewhere else to stay.

I do know an inn which is quite famous. I'm not going to name it because this is just me talking and others may have found it to be a splendid place. Not just one cased fish on the wall, but a line of them. Oak settles, grandfather clock, river over the meadow at the back and framed statements of praise from worthy magazines wherever else you looked.

But when the landlord asks you if you have had a good day, he looks over your shoulder when you reply. If you said you'd had only a 6 lb roach, he'd probably say, "Never mind, better luck tomorrow." And his idea of cheering you up would be heavy rain.

Sharing the experience of a good day, or even of a six-pound roach, must be done carefully. Don't do it in some drinking club, some 2CV and squash-racket palace, or in one of those hearty dens where you can't squeeze a quiet word round the bellies of Real Ale and Rugger spirit.

And sometimes I must say, though it hurts to admit it, even when you get real anglers around you as well as real ale, you can't get down to the serious stuff about tackle and the feel of it all. Any man who wants to do that is too clever by half, so you must fling the fivers over the bar and hear fishing stories which become fishing jokes, growing louder and louder until you realise that they are not about fishing at all. They're about high jinks which just happen to be by the river.

"What's wrong with that?", you ask. The answer is: absolutely nothing, except that fishing does seem to have become rather . . . well, bright and noisy, I suppose.

It is obvious that you are no more likely to fall in with strangers of like angling mind than you are to hook that six-pound roach the next time you try a new swim. Congenial company must be picked carefully and travelled with, thus turning every pub into a fishing inn. Otherwise it's a matter of luck – which makes fishing company different from fishing itself, because that contains only a small proportion of luck.

I turned in to my small and unassuming local the other day and realised that I like it because it isn't a fishing pub and I don't expect it to be one. In fact it's not an anything pub. Even golf is kept in its place – well, more or less. But the landlord has such gentlemanly charm that he really should have been an old fashioned angler.

Anyway, I turned in as usual for a pint, a pipe and a newspaper. In came a bearded stranger who was told that I'd been fishing that day. He asked, with proper humility, if I knew the river. He'd come down to fish it for the weekend.

Now you don't need me to warn you about this temptation. Anybody who asks advice about your home river is very likely to get it, at some length. And very shortly you see yourself as the gnarled old local in the corner – just

the sort of chap, in fact, that you've been seeking all over
the country.

Peculiar feeling, that. There's a lesson there
somewhere, though I can't force myself to consider it.

Well, I swear I kept the local lore short, stopping well
on the right side of pomposity. And he told me that he was
back from a week's fishing in Finland. He made Finland
sound like lakes and Sibelius, log cabins and locals who
talked fishing as if they'd nothing else to do. "Have you
seen their floats?", he said. No, I hadn't. What's more,
I'd never met anyone before with a working knowledge of
Finnish floats.

We talked floats, then. How they looked. How they
sat in the water. How they sank beneath the surface of
distant lakes shadowed by forests, mists and mosquitos.

After the last drink and the last tale, I never saw the
bearded visitor again. He was on his way back to some
city, some desk, some daily round far away. But the next
time I was in my pub, days later, the landlord said he had
something for me. From a shelf behind the bar he handed
me a float from Finland. With compliments from the man
with the beard the other night. Remember?

Indeed, I do remember. That float – slender, painted
impeccably in five colours – recalls for me not Finland so
much as the brethren of the angle who have not yet faded
away.

CHAPTER NINETEEN

Indulgence (1) . . . real sin

Of all the sins, collecting fishing tackle is known to be among the worst. It's all to do with greed, but we use a lot of arguments which sound good – and so become hypocrites as well as gluttons. Well, everybody knows that, doesn't he? Anglers have been warning about it for centuries. But as a new generation may have grown up since the last flurry of awful warnings and puritanical finger-wagging, I suppose it's all worth another airing.

If you want to understand, then you must start with Dame Juliana Berners. The first thing to learn about that lady, whose name has been spelt in various ways, is that she is mentioned so often by angling writers that you can feel a yawn beginning immediately. She keeps cropping up because a lot of people think she was the first angling writer, and to quote her gives you a feeling of having first-class credentials. Others keep rediscovering her, and feeling proud about it. Then that leads to fine rows because there are always a few thinking chaps who reckon that this fifteenth-century lady may not have said all the things attributed to her. Very soon now, someone is going to prove that she didn't exist at all and it was all done by that nameless monk who spent his time skiving down at the carp pond.

All right, I promise not to mention Dame Juliana again in this book, or Izaak Walton (more than a bit), or that Cromwellian trooper Richard Francke (who got a bit tired of Izaak, too), or all those Victorian fellows who could write today's lot under the table but, perhaps, not beat us with the rod.

Right, we are perfectly entitled to let the great ones rest while we get on with our own small affairs. In passing them, though, it's worth pointing out that they saw fishing as a healthy pursuit with a touch of grace. They told us to act like gents, observe the country code and say our prayers. In *The Boke of St Albans* you were told never to use the sport to increase your money, and it was taken for granted that anglers weren't covetous men in any way at all.

Well, times change and I reckon that many right worthy fysshinge folk of St Albans, or Winchester come to that, would have coveted hard if they'd had the money – or if the tackle trade had developed far enough to have its wits about it.

But let's assume, as Arthur Ransome did, that everything about angling in print took place in a nostalgic glow, and that things really were like that. Where does this leave people like me who gloat over piles of reels, for instance? Right at the bottom of the sin-bin, that's where.

The garden workshed has developed into the fishing-tackle shed and has been fitted with much more expensive locks than ever guarded "strimmers" and lawn-mowers – which have been banished to lesser accommodation.

There's one small mitigating point to set against all the black marks for self-indulgence – every item was acquired to do a job, it isn't there just to play with. I shall tell the ghostly anglers of the New Model Army, when they appear, accusingly, behind me that I'm a puritan at heart and all my stuff is on active service. Of course, some of it has been pensioned off to the reserve battalions, but that's fair enough. Surely nobody would expect me to bring into action the little black CAP fixed-spool reel which I had as a teenager? That one rests in honourable darkness at the back of a drawer with a broken spring, a missing screw and no hope of replacements. I remember the day when it had its guts ripped out by a pike whose screaming run against the clutch shattered the old soldier.

Anyway, I've used the handle to fit onto a French CrAck closed-face reel which, in turn, is made up of bits from a later companion, the CrAck 400. It seemed worthwhile getting the thing together, even through a Frankenstein job. The reel is unique. You disengage the concealed pick-up pin by a backward turn of the handle, and it's ready for casting. As with most closed-face reels, like the popular Abu, the CrAck suffers from line-bury. If you use these reels for moving water work then the coils bind into each other after a time – a major fault. Frankly I don't see why anyone should use this kind of reel at all, except as an alternative to the centrepin, for trotting. It should do that splendidly, after a bit of modification.

In fact, right now the Abu is up for adaptation in the shed. I've just been told that you have to increase the spool-spindle diameter by packing it with that plastic paste used for car bodywork repairs. Then you stick the spool in the chuck of an electric drill and round off the hardened mass with a chisel as it revolves. This seems worthy labour and, as we know, work is part of the puritan ethic.

Naturally I wouldn't lay a chisel, or a rough finger, on the Felton Crosswind. Like most of my gear it was second-hand, but anyone who knows anything about old reels will realise that this one cost hurting money. Again, though, I have an excuse ready. In boyhood, when everything fitted into a pocket or a flat cigarette tin, and the only rod was flourished and guarded better than the Standard at Naseby, I watched a master at work after bream.

While I stripped off coils of line from a tinny ''boy's reel'' and laid them on newspaper in order to cast a coffin lead to the middle distance, the master was bending gently over a netful of bronze bream. He added to the haul with a kind of easy regularity, taking his fish from under the opposite bank. It was so effortless, and I could see why. The soft click of a Felton Crosswind showed me how it was done.

From that day I coveted a Felton Crosswind. But that was the time when you saved even for hooks. That was when you mixed flour and water for bait; and if you broke your rod you repaired it, or never fished again. Obviously only those who lived in castles – or, at least, up stockbrokers' drives – could afford Felton Crosswinds. That was so many years ago that only men who were boys when I was a boy, and biked or bussed to their swims, can remember the reel. Long out of production. Long lost.

Yet I don't think that adolescent envy was misplaced. For me, the Felton was the best fixed-spool reel ever made but I must admit that the one I have now, after more than thirty years of waiting, has a drawback. It is the earliest Felton, which means it has a finger pick-up and not a full bale arm.

Much of my coarse fishing is done on fast rivers and therefore that business of uninterrupted line peel-off, once the run of the float begins, is all-important. This old Felton, cleaned up, oiled, adjusted and given love in its own cotton bag, is a delight to use . . . for a time. It is a pleasure to watch its remarkable action as the line comes back on the spool in perfect criss-cross pattern. But let the wind blow in the wrong direction or the strike be made at the wrong angle and suddenly you have two turns of line round the pick-up arm. That means trouble. That means cursing.

What is a practical collector to do? Well, obviously I shall need to seek out the later version of the Felton with full bale. That wouldn't be indulgence, just common sense.

With centrepin reels the issue is clearer and simpler. It's not easy to find a good reel of this type, and a man's a fool if he doesn't hold on to what he's got. If I'm any judge, fashion's swinging again and these reels are becoming trendy. Just wait and see.

Fortunately, I acquired a Young's Rapidex and a Trudex aeons ago, adding a Match Aerial rather later. Only last year I made a pilgrimage to Nottingham for the highly regarded Trentman special, which runs on ball races and weighs light on the rod. Now I'm thinking about trying a Swallow centrepin, since I've seen them being made. Well, that's how it goes with reels.

On his day, in the right conditions of wind and swim, the fisher with a centrepin is a monarch. All others on the river bank are servants in his hall. They may have the latest fixed spools, many of which appear to have fallen off the back of a Space Shuttle and carry so many garish twiddly bits (for trapping line at the wrong times) that you wonder if the fisherman needs to be there at all. Surely some of these reels could be computerised and do the whole job on their own, summoning their owners by bleep or radio, just to see what's been caught.

You have to pay heavily for revolving drums and put in a lot of effort learning how to use them. Until recently, people would do the first but not the second. Now that really *is* money talking without decent excuse.

I can't remember when I last saw a man make an F.W.K. Wallis Avon cast with a centrepin reel. Nowadays they'll climb up the rod, taking loops of line in their fingers and casting that way instead. It's impractical – worse, it's inelegant.

Or they'll peel off coils, as I did at the age of thirteen, and drop them on the grass. But someone, somewhere, is doing it the right way at this moment. His float is sailing out with grace and accuracy as mine does (sometimes). Last time I played the centrepin king, a couple of cynical observers were treated to the sight of the biggest bird's nest ever known on a river bank in more than thirty years of tackle-collecting.

CHAPTER TWENTY

Indulgence (2) . . . on the rack

If reels turn you towards indulgence, rods make you see how easily punishment may be given to the ardent collector. Have one or two in the corner, along with the yard broom and the deckchairs, and nothing can happen to you – except, of course, that rods stowed in that manner are going to get broken.

But march up and down a rank of thirty-three rods, rubbing your fat hands the while, and you know that you are in danger of making angling an acquisitive art rather than an active experience. And the day will come when you spend so long gloating that you never quite manage to leave the house.

The test should be – do you need every one of them? With thirty-three hanging in their bags the answer must be, of course, you darn well don't.

And yet (he feebly muttered) should you then throw away the first rod you ever owned, to make a start on the clearout? Ten feet of whole cane with a rather malleable built-cane top joint. No, I'm not going to do that. This rod is bowed with the weight of learning even more than with the weight of fish. The converted army tank aerial, my first leger rod, must stay to rust quietly away. Long ago it whipped in to three great chub on the Thames, one after the other, and until that day I'd felt nothing heavier than gudgeon and six-inch perch. You can still see how the chub bent it at the ferrule.

In past months I've been grafting quiver tips on to some of the glass rods, those with the length and taper that seem right for the job. But it's much more fun varnishing cane. Last night I took down the old James Avocet, with its whole-cane butt, split-cane middle and top. Originally a trotting rod – and always too short for the job – it has seen most service for rod-tip legering. Then there's the little Allcock 'Lucky Strike', different because it is all built cane, baked and brown and wandlike. These rods must have come from the period of traditional trotting when it was all done from punts. Now punts are as uncommon as built cane itself.

In any case, it has always been known that if you are going to run a float from the bank and take fish at a distance then you need a 12-foot rod at least, and 14-foot is better. Unless, of course, you have something like my Constable cane, Wallis Avon pattern, and still leaning forward when the choice is made.

A lot depends on the swim, I suppose. The best day's fishing I've had for some time was when I snatched the hours from 8 a.m. to noon with a Millwards Craftversa which, as far as I can see, was a product of the late fifties. Two-piece built-cane with slim handle on a reverse taper, it offered a lively feeling all the way along its 11 ft 3 ins. and was quite happy with the deep bankside swim.

I ran down a heavy Avon float with five AA shot and a lump of bread-flake on a no. 8 round-bend hook. The lot was backed up with stiff fistfuls of groundbait, bread and bran mix. And that, young man, is a system which was last heard of in the early fifties, too. With this sort of tackle in this sort of swim, the bites either come not at all or they are great, engulfing affairs. One moment the float is there, forging solidly downstream, and then it has gone. The rod's answer must be equally positive.

At whatever distance, five yards or twenty-five yards, the hook sank home and the cane responded to the hefty tug of three-pound chub. I had five like that and ten dace around the half-pound. There were some grayling and even, surprisingly, a minnow taken at extreme range on that mighty hook. Each time the action, the contact, the rushings and borings, were felt through the fingers and it felt safe. That's why yet another rod hangs in the shed and sometimes sees the light of day over river meadows.

My trout rods are mostly cane too, apart from something long, cheap and strong which I use for reservoir fishing and two passed on to me by a dear, dead friend. One of these gets a lot of use *in memoriam*, as it were. It was a sad duty to have to saw it open and glue in a bit of hollow tube after the original glass scrunched and crumpled in the butt section. Back in action again it is now, not as good as new, but once again capable of sending a fly quite sedately over narrow streams at least.

For serious dry-fly fishing on posh or difficult rivers the Sharp's 83 makes you sit up and smile. It does that even if your casting performance makes you want to sit down and groan. Here is sprightly impregnated cane with bounce and bonhomie. It's a delight just to carry it by the river and, though fearfully expensive at the time of purchase, is a luxury which has never caused any shock to the system.

Yet my best trout have come not on the back of this bright thoroughbred, but from the rather floppier exertions of another companion called an Aspindale's Perfection. Sadly, this one has lost its backbone and is now convalescing after majory surgery – glued and whipped two inches from the tip ring. But with it I have culled a hundredweight of rainbows and more, and one highly significant brownie, which came from an unfashionable place on an unknown river which had never seen a brownie before.

This was, I think, that legendary creature "the wild fish" which is almost unheard-of today, though people will often talk about having taken one so as to set themselves apart from the society of stockies. I shall avoid mention of his weight in case it seems to diminish the impact of the achievement. Better to say that I still see the moment under the trees, with the sun lying low on a bed of nettles and the solid fish showing his rosettes. And the fly coming away at a touch. The strike had been feeble and the old rod getting soft, even then. Yes, of course, I put the trout back.

Ranks of rods have memories as well as offering promise of more to come. They represent halcyon days. So where is the disadvantage really? Where is the penalty for the collector? What is the price of this armoury? Well, I'll try to tell you some more.

I lost a rod recently. Must have left it among the rhododendrons of some tench pond too public for comfort or honesty. The point is, though, that it took me days to discover that it had gone and while I was a bit sore about the matter, I reasoned that it wasn't much of a rod. Now if nobody thinks that is very terrible or at all meaningful, then they are quite right. It wasn't, but it should have been a tragedy.

It takes quite a time to pack for a day's fishing – and even longer to pack for a competition. This is not due to the care with which I scour, wash and cosset gentles, or to the effort I put into groundbait-mixing; nor is it to do with the way I nurture, select and prepare casters. I'm not much good at these things, which so occupy the time and trouble of skilful match fishers. No, the delay is due to being spoiled rotten for choice.

The canvas rod-roll holdall has eight compartments. Delete one for the brolly, another for the bundle which includes landing-net handle rod-rests, banksticks, and you have six spaces for rods. But which six rods?

A confident man, a pro-angler if you like, would not suffer this punishment. He would march to the rack and pick this and that, tie up his canvas roll and get away to the pub knowing all's ready for the morning.

Lesser anglers, like me, pace up and down. Small irritations emerge, since you can't remember which rod is in which bag. Once, I decided to break out of this silly business and pack one leger rod and one long float rod. When I got to the water I found that the long rod had no tip ring – it was one of those awaiting repair. Naturally that was the day that I drew from the hat an absolutely perfect float-fishing peg.

Many a fisherman on his way to building up quite an array of rods will still wonder what on earth I'm on about. Many a hard-eyed and humourless egalitarian individual of leftward persuasion will ask why I don't dispose of this self-created problem by distributing my rods to the deserving poor and the unemployed. Well, the reason why I don't is that I might be unemployed myself one day, since it happens even to anglers. Then I'll have an auction. But even then I won't let them all go. I'll hang on to one or two nostalgic ones and the Sharp's 83, and the 14-foot Hardy "Thames Style", just in case float-flickering roach fishing comes back again.

And I'd better keep the 14-foot CTM, not because it's nice but because it does the job better than cane of similar length. And the Peter Stone glass leger rod. And the salmon rod. And the Sealey 13-foot Aquarius, because it's worth nothing but somehow copes with a variety of situations surprisingly well.

After that I shall find that there's nothing much left to sell which is worth the price of advertising or the services of an auctioneer. So I'll keep the lot and get rid of the lawnmowers instead.

CHAPTER TWENTY ONE

Indulgence (3) . . . trapped!

It had to happen, and it has. Here was my favourite tackle-shop owner doing his stuff again. "You ought to move to carbon, Phil", he said. He's been calling me Phil for ten years now, and never seems to notice that he gets a different set of initials on my cheques.

I lifted the rod. It felt too good, so I put it down again. This has been a weekly ritual. He looked round the shop and addressed the usual loiterers – all of whom have, of course, owned carbon rods for years. "It's a challenge to get him to buy one", he said.

They looked politely baffled. Couldn't understand someone who had only moved to the very edge of the Carboniferous period, which had been in for so long.

"Can't afford it", I said.

"Course you can", he said. "This one is second-hand."

"Don't need it", I said.

"Look, just try it again, take it for a week and bring it back if you don't want it", he said.

I remind you that this is a ritual, but that doesn't make it an empty game. Nobody *needs* a carbon rod. Just as nobody really *needed* a glass-fibre rod – but now I have three of them for bottom fishing.

I bought the first from Woolworth's without telling anyone. Why did I do that? Don't ask me – I think it was embarrassment. A bit like buying contraceptives from a crowded supermarket rather than from a quiet chemist. It's over before anyone notices.

When I got that Woolworth's rod home I took out a tin of white paint and gave it a name. I wrote just above the handle "Decadence 1". When I acquired two more rods in glass I called them "Decadence 2" and "Decadence 3". That's the kind of thing that can happen to people who try to be sensible about consumer durables. And why did I buy glass rods at all? Even if you're slinking backwards to decay you don't quite lose your inquisitiveness.

As you will have understood by now, provided you haven't lost patience, I use cane rods quite often, as well as cane seat baskets and centrepin reels. Dave, the tackle shop man, knows this and approves, because he is of my generation and much more of a person than a profit-seeker. The other day he unearthed a certain fixed-spool reel of astonishing ugliness called an Omnia, once his pride and joy. He knew that once it was mine, too.

Before entering the shop like a dinosaur caught up in this era, I had been fishing with Decadence 2, having broken Decadence 1 while punch-casting towards the next county. In a club match, with fish hard to come by, I'd lost two chub, which sort of bumped off the hook.

Up came the club secretary to tell me that it wouldn't have happened if I'd been using carbon. Carbon would win all the time. Carbon would make me a better fisherman. Carbon hadn't made *him* a better fisherman, because he was good enough already, but it had lightened his holdall. Just one rod he carried now, for everything, and look what it had done for him. I almost asked him if he knew the tackle dealer called Dave (he does actually, but I'm sure there was no collusion there).

Well, if Decadence 2 was a symbol of degeneration and Decadence 1 had given up . . . was it worth getting out Decadence 3, anyway? Time for a pipe and an examination of motives and wallet.

The next weekend I was due to put a float over the Test for grayling – and when those ladies start corkscrewing in the current at the end of a long line you soon know whether your rod has the hooking power or not. For that day I took one of the last cane rods Dave sold me – a Constable which bends so sweetly, if a little heavily, to the fin. We did well together. Why ask for more?

But, you see, he forgets all this when I go into his shop. Just carries on slowly turning it over entirely to the Carboniferous period. But he hasn't been having it all on his side of the counter. Some of us has-beens can do more than make negative shrugs when under sales pressure.

You should have heard me putting on my grandfatherly quaver and muttering about bolts from the blue striking the carbon man before he can strike the fish. I said that those rods should have lightning conductors attached to them and be tested for a kite mark.

At the time I said that, a man in the shop was being thoughtful about a carbon reservoir rod with a profitable-looking price tag. I think Dave already had the till open. But the customer put the rod back and wandered off. Well, perhaps he hadn't really meant to buy it.

As far as I can see, cane has weight, energy, style; and glass is light but spongy by comparison. This is, of course, an illusion – provided it's good glass – due to old hands and closed minds. But certainly glass is a bit thick in section and gets pushed around in the wind.

Still, these are old, old matters, sorted out long ago and argued over no longer. I only mention them again for historical reasons and because glass is going the way of cane. The thing I keep saying, though, is that the fish still look the same.

"The fish still look the same, Dave", I said.

"Give you that", he said, looking wise.

I also said that in the days when people were underfed and died at thirty, they still managed to fish with hefty poles and whalebone, and all that. What was wrong with us that we had to have featherweight rods in order to be in the swim?

There was a man, once, who wore a Woodbine on his lips and a collar stud on his shirt. He was not wearing a stovepipe hat as well, but his rod was something huge in mottled cane and lancewood. He was putting a float downstream and baiting with elderberries. The roach he caught still spring out at me in rosy light, on red fins. He had dozens. Then he let this boy hold the rod for two swims down – I can recall exactly. And I had a roach each time. It didn't seem to me that the great rod was any sort of handicap.

"That rod didn't bother him, Dave", I said.

There was a pause. Then a fill of tobacco. Then another pause. I paid him the second-hand price for the traded-in carbon 12-footer, and he wiped a tear from his eye as he took the money.

Do you know, the damn thing's a pointing finger, an extension of hand, arm and brain. It's prim, it's precise – it practically beckons the fish and they come quietly. I do hope I'm not going to have to start rod-collecting all over again.

CHAPTER TWENTY TWO

Freezer fodder

Talk about being clobbered with warning signs. I was punching out a long line towards something like half the distance everybody else was managing (as usual) and found I was thinking about the freezer.

It's a new freezer, and I should have been thinking about a new rod instead. The nine feet of elderly cane I was using had developed a neat gap around the keeper-ring. Just cracked varnish? Ailing binding only? Well that's just what I said until my ear picked up the creaking noises. Now I use that as an excuse for not being able to cast far enough.

But there was no excuse for thinking about the freezer. The chap next to me wasn't thinking about a freezer as he beat upwind close-hauled on the starboard tack, or whatever his casting technique is called.

And the man beyond him, with a hat so loaded with large flies that it lifted with each passing breeze like an insecurely held kite – well, he was so grim I knew what he was thinking. Back at the hut somebody he doesn't like very much had just put something rather impressive in the fishing book.

Which just left me with my confession to make. It came like this.

First, I was twitching about with a nymph on the edge of a ripple. I've rationalised my flybox and in the rationalised half it is now crammed with these particular nymphs. That means confidence. Round about the fourth twitch I slumped into some figure-of-eighting then . . . pluck, bang . . . curse! And confidence shattered. Hardly felt him! I howled backwards in a sigh through my teeth. The others didn't hear me.

Not wanting to make a fuss, I reeled-in and secretly examined ten feet of tapered knotted leader which had taken time to make. It was now six feet of knotted leader. At that point I should have gone in for the rapid bit of self-analysis all proper rainbow men do if they want to see the colours again. All right, I was fishing too fine. All right, the weight of the line in the water gave him a brick wall to pull against. All right, I was too tight to the rod tip . . .

That's what I started to say. Then I thought about the economic situation instead. The freezer is part of it. They say that you can save money by filling it up, and your limit of rainbows takes a nice lot of space in the thing.

Before I leave to go fishing, the freezer is humming a kind of hungry song. When I come back it either gives a satisfied gurgle and slurp, or snarls. It depends on how much I've caught. Lose a single rainbow because of damn bad fishing and somewhere back there a red light flicks on.

It's all a bit like the old jokes coming true. One's wife was part of the old jokes but, in pre-freeze days, you could laugh. The man coming through the door with a sprat in his hand was greeted with arms akimbo and something witty and devastating. Or with a rolling pin.

Now, it's different. Now, if he carries two rainbows of 2 lb apiece he has failed, because it's not just the cat who waits any more, it's 16 cubic feet of cold, expensive space with food prices rising all around it.

As it happens, I find that on most of the waters I fish I can do as well with my short line as others do with their long ones, but the pride of success doesn't hit me so hard as the horror of failure. And that's not just bad, it's very significant.

With rainbows, how many of us are fishing for the freezer? Have rainbows become mere freezer fodder? Or is it just me . . . lost like the lover of pornographic sex who did everything and found there was nothing left to excite him?

I've been praising all those men who are digging holes in the ground and filling them with rainbows. Honestly and seriously, we can't do without them. But the essence of put-and-take is hard calculation, or everybody's in trouble.

And this rubs off on the happy anglers who are there for the take. For all I know, many a man has been pushed over his limit by the thought of a freezer waiting at home. After all, it's only a small step towards casting financial calculations. If I pay so much for one day a week and take my limit two days out of four . . . let me see . . . with trout costing so much a pound I'll cover my costs in . . .

I know a traditional trouter who reckons this kind of thinking makes you no better than professional match fishermen. Not that I listen to this kind of talk; but the wound festers, just the same.

Yet with all these rainbows about, hard-fighting splendid fellows that they are, and men designing pellet-flies, I find we are getting to think of the fish as so much useful flesh only. Meanwhile, of course, back at the freezer centres, you can buy packs of undersized rainbows for not much more than the cost of good catfood.

I worried so much about all this that I let a rainbow go after unhooking him. He was around three pounds. No, naturally I didn't let anybody see me do it. I'd have been frowned on as much as if they'd seen me broken. I let him go as a last dying fling in favour of the old order, when catching a good fish was a surprise. Know what I mean?

Yet, when I unhooked him and hoped that exhaustion wouldn't make nonsense of the gesture, I felt a small ache in my wallet. I went on to placate the looming freezer by taking my limit and was one short when the last fish turned up and amazed me. I'd been flashing around in the depths and stripping myself into weariness (look with scorn on that, it's a sure sign of freezer slavery) when I felt guilty and replaced the Butcher (bloody thing).

In the Butcher's place I tied on a weighted nymph of delicious shrimp-like form. Out with it and start thinking in the old way. After a time a picture of what I was doing on the bottom came into my mind. With the old satisfaction I fished with small lifts, small movements, gentle, careful, slow, delicate.

My strike, when it came, bit into something that was not flamboyant, it was just heavy. It didn't thrum and quiver in the long rainbow dash. It didn't boil with power so as to break into air in a smash of water droplets. Instead it fought below, doggedly, out of sight, and my wrist ached. I thought it was a coarse fish (there, in part, lies the last non-commercial angling, anyway) and then he weakened and I won.

No pale line of blushing mauve, no spattering of small specks. He bore rich rosettes; he was the fish nobody had put in and nobody knew was there. A brownie living down among the water snails and somehow immune from Tandems and Hairies and devilish Rosses and bloody Butchers.

I wanted to put him back, as well, with a kind of salute to fading sensations. But the freezer waited, and I had my limit to consider.

CHAPTER TWENTY THREE

Sunburned sportfishers

Next trout season I may open on the Upper Avon or the Wylye. The big decision depends on all sorts of factors . . . like wind and weather in relation to the beats you can get on the club tag system. That's when your choice of fishing day is dictated by how many bits of numbered plastic are left on the board in the hedge by the time you get there.

But mainly the choice will be due to simple, instinctive things. Shall it be a small water with small, rather difficult fish or shall it be the broader, deeper flow with bigger fish but the danger of having someone else fishing on the opposite bank?

One thing is pretty obvious, though: I shall not be casting over the boiling Rio Grande that runs into St Margaret's Bay, Jamaica.

There are bold and sunburned travelling anglers who know the feel of weighty fish in mighty waters. Deferentially, I nod to them and fall silent when they speak. You meet them in departure lounges at airports. They wander idly by, rod cases under their arms and worldly looks on their faces, while you are struggling to find your boarding card. These people seem to be something other than anglers. Perhaps they are sporting rodsmen. Certainly they show their internationalism by referring to "sportfish" and "sportfishing" (one word, in each instance), and though they swear that they are just as happy potting dace on black gnats in some English sidestream, I don't think this can be true.

The bamboo rafts that carry Caribbean tourists down the Rio Grande or the Martha Brae river do not pass many fishermen. As you surge down the rapids and swing round the bends a small black figure might be seen standing in the buzzing heat with a bamboo pole in his hands, but you can never find anyone who knows what kind of fish he is expecting to catch. Well, only an angler would ask, but I doubt if even a sportfisher would know without looking it up in his notebook. Even the West Indians don't seem to go in for freshwater fishing all that much.

Sitting under my straw hat, I threw a few thoughts around. Angling potential? New line for visitors? The tourist board people seemed interested if a little puzzled. Surely, they said, it would be better to fish in the sea. Plenty of fish in the sea. Better fish, too. But sea fishing, like sportfishing, is something else, and I was wondering what wet-fly tackle might do in the burning cockpit country of Jamaica where the Martha Brae hides on the edge of jungly hillocks and it's all very wild, man. Or might legered luncheon meat be better?

On that trip I had no rod with me and no time to walk the banks anyway. There was Port Antonio just down the road and a general travel piece to write, as well as a lot of rum to drink. Nobody else in the hotel was a sportfisher anyway, so I couldn't borrow so much as a hook.

That's how we miss our chances. What mightn't a day on the brown water have shown me? Frankly, I don't feel deprived, though. Give me a week there, and I reckon I might get a bit of local knowledge and haul something out. But it would probably be something nasty and snappy, with bulges in the wrong place and a sting in the tail.

Another year produced a short burst of snorkelling in Tobago, lolling in the lee of a great reef. Exotic fish lay around in pockets of weed and coral. Entrancing. Utterly absorbing. But this was alien beauty, and you feel it's really nothing much to do with you. Like the sand, the sun and the steel drums, those fish were not real, not like trout and roach. Back at the boat, if someone had offered me tackle and bait I wouldn't have wanted to use them: I'd have felt as if I were taking part in that fairground game, attempting to catch metal fish with magnets. Fish in another world. Something apart from angling.

For different reasons, I ducked an invitation to go for catfish in the USA. Catfish aren't beautiful like parrot fish, say, and it's hardly their fault. But I can't imagine anyone wanting a great, gaping, sinuous, heaving lump like that on the end of his line.

Yet sportfishers don't have such qualms. Perhaps real anglers don't, either, to judge by the way some have welcomed the introduction of catfish to certain British waters. Which may mean that I'm not a real angler, after all.

Any man in shorts and baseball cap who grins beside a carcass suspended from a vast butcher's hook has the pride of the hunter about him, but it makes a poor picture – unless the aim is to advertise cold-store facilities. On a smaller scale, those who stick fingers in the gills of rainbows and hold them up to the lens (out towards the lens actually, because they look bigger that way) seem to be holding just so much sagging meat.

From all this jabbing at others, sour-grapishly as it were, I guess that for some of us fishing is a ritual, even a chauvinistic ritual. It is toying with the familiar rather than execution of the exotic. Of course, there may be nobody else out there like me. Who's this bloke who likes his thrills in measured doses and homely places? Wouldn't he prefer to cut his way to the river through sugar cane and tropical fern, rather than through the hopfields of Kent?

Yet what is it to me that I know nothing of mahseer in India, when I still have to discover how to catch mullet in English estuaries? New experiences may be waiting over the sea, but my hands are full with what awaits me round the next curve of the Stour. There's no time for far horizons because that would be time stolen from attainable excitement.

So, next season I may go to the Wylye; but the last one opened for me on the Otter. Strange little stream that, and inviting, until it leaks away over a strip of gravel at Budleigh Salterton.

I snatched three hours from a business weekend with nobody else about on the water, apart from a walking lady with Yorkshire Terriers and one visiting angler by the bit of wire across the river which marks the tidal limit. On the other hand it could merely have been a barrier to cows or something.

The little river was fast in places, with some surprising stickles of the brisk sort, but also some slow, deeper sections. It was good to wade a bit and flop around with an old three-piece cane 9-footer – "Lockfast" ferrules and all. After breaking on the strike to a decent little tug at the nymph (no, not the over-powerful rod, but a badly blood-knotted leader) I then missed two other takes, owing entirely to thoughtless fishing.

The holiday angler packed up and said he always found maggots best, anyway. I was wondering about that for the next blank hour, but finding maggots in a Devonshire April is as difficult as finding freshwater hooks in Jamaica. Anyway, during that hour nothing moved and nothing was seen, apart from a slinky mink which slid onto a boulder and watched me for a time.

The dog lady came back and asked if I was after mullet. Just a bit early for them wasn't it, I said. She didn't know. But it seems that this particular stretch of the Otter was for mink and mullet with a sea-trout bonus later on. There were no rules to speak of, so a wading man with a fly rod was just out to handicap himself.

Before getting back to the conference hall I had a last cast downstream of a line of boulders and disturbed two baby flounders that rose above the toes of my waders like waterlogged leaves left over from autumn. As far as I am concerned, that was an exotic experience. Here was I, nymphing in mullet water and waving a fly rod over flounders. Nothing in the Martha Brae or the Mississippi could have felt so strange or so interesting. Some of us are happy with small things.

Some weeks afterwards I was looking over a man's fishing tackle; he had advertised it for sale. We sat on a kitchen table in a suburban bungalow and he said he was home from South Africa, where he'd fished a lot, but was hooked on gardening now. He was short, stocky, bald and bespectacled. He had angled in distant places but showed no trace of bronzed skin, no faraway sportfisher's gaze in his eyes. Yet his tackle spoke for him.

It was in a black japanned metal doctor's box, with a leather handle. There were three folding compartments painted white inside. His spools of nylon were pale blue and American. There was a pile of plugs larded with Uncle Sam's coarse trebles. Ancient paper packets of leaders imported from the House of Hardy lay beside a container made of mottled Bakelite. Inside that were springs, screws and spindles from long-dead reels, all hoarded against the day when, no doubt, running repairs might be needed out where the hyenas howl.

There was also a Young's no. 2 Ambidex fixed-spool reel with all parts in place. He looked at it with a glimmer of love.

"That's seen some fish", he said.

"I'll bet it has", I said.

We looked at each other. But instead of a traveller's tale about epic struggles far from your tamed and decent English buttercups, he just said "Fiver for the lot".

I took the surgeon's field-box home and replaced the hooks on the plugs for some which were more suitable and English. The Ambidex groaned a bit and the handle turned stiffly. I took it apart for a thorough cleaning, and found that the bearings were choked with sandy grit. It was dark red grit. Not Devonian red from the banks of the Otter, but something – you could so easily imagine – from the floor of the high veldt.

That reel is still in use. It runs sweetly now, and only occasionally do I wonder about its performance in other days and other places.

CHAPTER TWENTY FOUR

Don't take it so heavy, dearie

The other morning there was John Arlott on the radio looking back to the great days of cricket and football. Anybody who doesn't know who John Arlott is must surely be reading this so many years hence that we're all in the past tense. So don't worry about it, poor citizen of 2000 AD, just go back to your wallpaper videoscreen because you won't know what I'm talking about.

John Arlott, in retirement, said he'd lost interest in football because the crowds, the times and the players had also lost interest in the game – at least in the game he knew. They were all up to something different. This made me wonder if fishing will seem like that to some of us one day – enough to make a man hang up his rods as others might hang up their boots.

That idea comes like a cold wind on the back of the neck. But if you look at what has been done to a silly old thing called sportsmanship, then what are we to make of the effect of mail order houses on tackle shops? Or what the water authorities have done to rivers? Or what the farmers have done to waterside meadows?

You don't have to go far to come across those who fish in teams, wearing a uniform which they call a "strip", with an oriental tacklemaker's name on the back of the plastic jacket and also on a baseball cap. Best wishes to them, the future is theirs . . . but thank the Lord it's not

happening just down the road from my place, where I can
still find a man fishing high-speed current with an
unsuitable porcupine quill. That's also where an idle if
rather attractive daydreamer hooked a chub of more than
6 lb on two dead maggots circulating in an eddy. What's
more, she landed it.

On this water, a man from the time of Stanley
Matthews (remember his name, you out there in the 21st
century?) can still show the heaviest net of chub and
grayling and the younger ones can still marvel and listen
and be envious without worrying too much about doing
better.

No, it's nothing to do with some island where time
stands still, it's purely a matter of luck and numbers. The
fishing is restricted to a hundred anglers or so. As simple
as that – or as profound, if you're interested in things like
social engineering. The luck comes in because we seem to
have a hundred good fellows, though some may not
necessarily think that about me. It's even luckier that no
more than five or six of them seem to go fishing on the
same day.

Yes, thing have changed for the worse generally, but
I bet you can judge the quality of a fishing situation without
even mentioning fish. Like saying that you may go for a
pint at lunchtime without packing up, and your tackle will
still be there when you get back. Well, seven times out of
ten that will happen.

On the bridge, regarding this little lot of paragons in
March, I was shifting from boot to boot in deep cold. No
snow. No frost. Just dull coldness helped along by
something coming up rather briskly across the meadows
from the north-east.

The best swim on this reach is just by some posts and
wire at the end of the first field downstream from the bridge
(not that this means much to you, thanks be, or every

blighter who reads this would be queuing up – and it won't be the best swim in the 21st century, anyway, because they'll have abolished the river by then).

As I say, then, on this bitter day I was watching this swim and waiting for something to happen. Since I wasn't fishing, and had one of my dogs with me anyway, it was up to somebody else to make it happen while I held on to the lead. Nobody did.

There was a man in this swim-to-beat-all-swims who told me he'd been fishing another famous – if rather muddier – river for days and had taken nothing. Now he was on this far nicer stretch of water to renew his confidence in angling.

Just one chub would've done it for him. So we watched his float sweeping down on the river's grey back. My bitch even barked encouragingly at it. But no chub came. For something to do, he changed his float. But we knew that this meant nothing. There are times when you are sure that the thing will never go under. Which, of course, is when it does. Just once, in several hours, his float went under.

He struck, felt a judder and a plunge . . . and the rod was suddenly light in his hand again with the wind blowing up his sleeve.

Of course, he'll be back in that swim again next week, or next season, or some time. At least, I hope he'll think that perseverance is worthwhile. I know what the chubless one meant by needing to renew his confidence in the game. However, I fear that if he fails too often he might take up golf instead, or say cynical things about fishing, on the radio. Not that golf will do anything for his confidence. Everybody says that you can't fish and play golf, anyway. Golf is not a second pleasure to anything, it's a deadly disease.

As it happens, our local golfing doctor was a fisherman once. He confessed to me one pubby evening that he hung up his rod for ever after a splendid day after Scottish trout in his home glen. His wasn't quite like John Arlott's case. The game hadn't changed and disheartened him. It didn't happen on a poor day. Not on a cold day . . . but a fine, successful day. He said he suddenly realised that he didn't care if he caught the next trout or not. So he never tried again.

He also alleges that he doesn't care that much whether he wins over 18 holes or not. But since he talks enough with other clubmen about not winning, it is clear that he is in the same position as a bloke who talks about not catching chub on impossible days in March. Which means that the doc will go on driving and putting for ever, and it couldn't happen to a nicer chap.

I am determined that something of that sort shall not happen to me, though the danger is there. I've just taken up golf, actually. At the moment I'm just sort of teetering before the black hole, so to speak. After a few lessons the pro is wondering if he should go on taking my money.

There was one round the other week when the golfing doctor and kindly friends somehow got me through to the 18th – even carrying my bag once or twice when I was taking rather long to plough my lonely furrow towards a flag on the hill.

Our local course has water hazards left there by nature, not by the architect. Thrashing towards one of the streams I found that, as usual, it had risen up and swallowed my ball. The others were ahead – again, as usual – and I was wondering why I bothered to play this game. Perhaps I was just pausing to rest my arms, which were throbbing after hammering the good earth so many times. Anyway, whatever the reason, I looked at the clear water in this ditchlike streamlet not at all as keen golfers do.

For golfers, bird watchers, ramblers and other lesser souls whose pleasure takes them near water, it is a matter of looking at it rather than into it. But as I looked for the ball I noticed small darting minnows. Then there was a pointed flash under water which directed my eye to the ball nestling on gravel. As I went on my knees to get it, the perspective was altered and the tiny stream became a river with bends, deeps, shallows and twistings round the roots of old trees. As I stayed still, the minnows came back. And among them, tucked into six inches of bend below an eighteen-inch glide, was a miniature troutling.

Voices sounded on the fairway, making helpful noises in golfing language. I reached for the underwater ball and got up "He's found it at last", someone said.

Very correctly, I dropped the ball exactly one club-length from the hazard. Then I whacked it in the general direction of the green and rejoined the other world like a man who has left an old friend behind.

In fact, fishermen and golfers are similar creatures. You can make just as much of a mess with a no. 8 iron as you can with an 8-foot trout rod.

I've often noticed chaps slinking away with bags on wheels at 6 a.m. – just as I passed with a vaguely similar bag containing rods. They did it for the same reasons, too. Golf courses are crowded places, like river banks. You don't get up early to find a good swim: you do it to have any kind of swim. On the first tee in the early morning the course stretches ahead of you just as a fine river does. It's the surroundings that count as much as the game. At least that's what golfing literature says and has been saying since the days of plus-fours and hickory shafts.

Golf talk is like fishing talk. Here's the doc at an inquest round the bar – ribbing in a kind of dryly lairdish fashion. The landlord, who has humped his clubs back in double-quick time in order to open up, sparkles with triumph and disaster.

The regulars inch closer along what is already one of Britain's shorter bar surfaces. That dog leg on the 15th . . . a no. 3 wood took him over the oak from the tee . . . and you know how the ball runs off left near the rough on the hump above the ditch near the holly bush . . .

Blink an eye and think of fishing talk. That gravel bar in the third meadow . . . a first-time chuck with a weight-forward had the fly sitting up nicely for the fast run on the opposite bank . . . you know how the drag gets you by that old willow . . .

It's about three-and-a-half miles round our local course as the rabbit runs, and about the same to do a day's work on the nearest trout stream. Seems to me that fly-fishing on a rough, tough water with long beats or, better still, no beats at all, is about the same as golf on the energy expenditure table. But on the cursing level, golf just nudges ahead. Kneeling on thistles below the shallows, it isn't impossible to lose track of the short line is it? Until a tug behind you says that the fly is in the willow. Three times that happened to me at a certain spot. Three flies lost. Three shapes speeding away to weed. Three distinctive short snorts from me, with pointed words on the end of them.

In the local golfing circle they still nod understandingly at the man who came in with obvious thoughts of suicide. Inconsolable he was. Bought nobody a drink. Said he'd give up golf. Whether it was his putting or his slice nobody now remembers. But since the same chap later made more of a name by playing two notable rounds of 18 in one day separated only by a significant amount of good ale, it is considered that he is now over his trauma.

When a fisherman bodges it, he doesn't sob into his pint. But if he quietly goes away to buy some clubs, spiked shoes and the discipline of keeping his head still, he'd better be sure to get his mental attitude right. No, not just so that he can hit the ball, but so that he doesn't let his rods grow cobwebs in the garage.

"Suppose you'll be giving up fishing now?" people say to you. There are almost as many golfers as fisherman, I'm sure, so people say that quite a lot. Now I'm not saying it couldn't happen – after all, it happened to the doc. But I am saying that it can be a damned close-run thing. What I have noticed about golf is that while you may be playing against the course (just as you fish against the river), you are always anxious to get a move on. That is definitely a minus-factor in the balance of pleasures.

There's always someone coming up behind you and he's always a better player. No time to admire your most unusual stroke that went click, and lifted fair and square rather than going slap and bouncing along the ground. No time to discuss with your partner the fall of shot. No, it's up with the trolley and on to the next hole, because they're getting close behind.

During a good fishing day you can get the sense that the river is yours. The golf course is never yours. It is beautiful, but speckled with moving figures making themselves felt over hundreds of yards. True, you may stop for a second to hear the cuckoo, and you can wave others through. But there's less urgency about recovering a Spring Olive from the bushes, or mixing the next dollop of groundbait. Certainly we all need a fillip in the region where confidence lurks. To get it back after a series of inept performances on stream or green is important. But there are only two ways to go. More practice, or laying off for a time.

More practice means more casting (or swinging) and laying off means no casting (or swinging). If you are caught in the middle of these problems then something may have to go. Shall it be the clubs or the rods?

As the good Rabbi said, shortly after John Arlott had been on the radio: "Don't take it so heavy, dearie." Had he been talking about golfing fishermen he would have saved his breath.

Oddly enough, the doc looked hard at his slimline tonic the other evening and, before putting something interesting in it, was heard to say he was wondering if he might take up fishing again.

CHAPTER TWENTY FIVE

Shopping for porky barbel

There was this man from a suburb in Dorset (a county which really shouldn't have suburbs at all), who said he'd just been fishing on the Stour. Not entirely amazing, that, since everybody must surely fish the Stour at least once before they die.

But this happy man was fishing for the first time in his life, so you must be respectful becuse the first time is always the best. However, he had a problem and it was puzzling him. The bait kept coming off the hook, he said. What bait was he using? He said oh, just the usual, same as everyone else.

Careful questioning showed that he'd been on luncheon meat. As soon as they heard about this all the anglers of Wessex nodded wisely. Of course they've been opening tins for years, like everybody else, and told this chap that you've got to use the right brand of meat in the Stour as in any other river. And naturally you mustn't cast weight and bait like a golfer driving for the horizon. As it happens, this chap is a golfer . . . which is why he didn't deserve to catch a 3 ½ lb chub on his luncheon meat – and at pretty nearly the first attempt, too. Such things should happen only after long and earnest apprenticeship and much failure.

So those who have waited weeks for their first reasonable chub wouldn't actually rush to tell him much about such tricks as impaling a caster upon the hook so that it rests against the hunk of meat, between it and the barb, and acts as a kind of shock-absorber for it in flight. The bed of the Stour in this particular spot (and elsewhere, no doubt) must be like a display counter at the supermarket. This is probably why all the big barbel look like pork butchers.

Last time I asked, the best barbel taken there were reaching 11 lb – two fish at that weight and one weighing in at 10 lb 3 oz. By now the luncheon-meat feast has probably added a further half-pound at least.

If it isn't luncheon meat, though, it's probably sweet corn. On most days anywhere you will find people who like to carpet the bottom with corn. You'd think the stuff was some kind of cash crop, but often it delivers the goods, earning you a pile of notes at a local match with perhaps half a dozen chub and something even heftier to go with them. At least, that is the hope as jolly anglers turn green with envy at the next man's giant fish. So, before the next cast, in with the tinned corn again as loose-feed.

I took a brace of trout recently, and each fish had the yellow grains literally falling out of its mouth – a wonder that they took the little green nymph I threw at them. Perhaps they thought it had fallen out of the tin by mistake.

I know that these are scarcely exotic baits nowadays and wouldn't mention them at all except to wonder why they haven't been banned yet – or to see if they are going to be banned tomorrow.

Banning things is quite well known as an angling activity, owing, no doubt, to the fact that some anglers aren't happy, comradely chaps at all. Every now and then we produce shambling ones – usually in Hong Kong para jackets – who like to throw sweet-corn tins or luncheon-meat tins into the river once they have fed the fish and feel like going home. Oh well, put that caustic opinion down to my deprived formative years, when a tin of Spam was a treasure to be guarded and shared and probably came in a food parcel.

Take hempseed instead. It doesn't come in tins but is still frowned on in some quarters and has been banned at one famous Dorset fishery since 1965. Yet not far away, the rules of a local anglers' association who have a highly-regarded fishery on the Avon, are now liberalised. At one time they labelled the little black seed as a "noxious substance". Despite all the rows and all the writings going on for years, this attitude was widespread. It was probably true only to the extent that the stuff is thought to rot on the bottom of the river when the fish have grown tired of trying to mop it up. But to those who draft rule books, there was the feeling that using hemp might cause them to come across a chub or a roach hallucinating quietly in a corner.

Fish that manage to find their way past the hillocks of hempseed do, of course, come across the supreme bait, which is still the maggot. There were howls and learned articles in fishing journals when they banned the maggot from the most famous fishery in Britain, which happens to be at Christchurch – and so the ban was lifted a few seasons ago. Nothing very terrible has happened, so far as I'm aware.

Since maggots now cost around £1 a pint (a measure that takes sawdust as well), and since very fine experts or very decadent men like to turn up with a gallon of them, it's surprising that the economy of the market-place hasn't forced its own ban upon us. Certainly some fishery managers report that people aren't as liberal with the maggots these days, since it is a bit like scattering handfuls of fivepenny pieces before fish.

Wessex waterkeepers (and all others) don't just ban baits, though . . . they also ban people who face the wrong way at the riverside. Fly fishers from the best of the Wiltshire clubs, who cast in a forbidden direction, can be ordered away, never again to pollute with their presence the banks of Avon or Wylye. The downstream cast with your fly is seen as worse than tipping a whole supermarket trolleyful of luncheon meat tins into the shining stream.

It must be said that this club believes that it is keeping faith with the ancient art of fly fishing. They have their instincts in the right place, but in this they are wrong, since the distinguished giants who fished Test and Itchen, wearing elegant suits and writing all the source-books, wouldn't have agreed at all.

As it happens, all this is in a good cause (ensuring that you don't catch too many expensive stock trout), although it is a fact that fishing a dry fly downstream is devilishly difficult – which is probably why upstream fly fishing was invented.

Still, rules are rules and when a quiet and determined figure stood and watched me for at least ten minutes I couldn't argue when he came up to have a word with me, playing it by the clock.

"I agree that you didn't drop back past twelve o'clock most of the time", he said.

"Good", I replied, thinking this was quite an achievement, given that the rise was under the opposite bank in a fast rip of current and with certain bushes very badly placed indeed.

"But I saw you touch 11 o'clock on two occasions", he said. He sounded hurt.

Being one who never quite sees trout streams in chronological terms, even when range-finding, all I could think of to say was sorry, won't do it again, my watch must have been wrong. Very kindly, he let me off. And, of course, the trout lived to rise another day.

Even if you applaud bans on certain evil human activities, nobody would go so far as to approve of banning the dace. Somehow this seems to have happened naturally in parts of the middle Avon. A year or two ago this fine and gallant little fellow turned up all over the place. He and his many mates made sure that few anglers had fishless days. But now, while you can still catch a few, ''The Mystery of the Missing Dace'' has become a talking-point.

Ask the water authority, and its experts reckon that the dace is abundant in the area. They are too gentlemanly to suggest that maybe anglers aren't working hard enough these days. Wouldn't do them much good if they did say that – we know what we know. The watermen's suggestion is that daceless patches might be occurring as a result of one of nature's little mysteries, which nobody can afford to explore just at the moment.

Well, that may be. Only some Hampshire anglers think that the dace have gone because of the billowing cubic tonnes of excreta and suspended protein from the trout farms. Or is it that dace don't like barbel? Certainly the barbel population exploded as the dace declined. Like dace, they spawn on gravel. What's more, I'm told that they spawn a month or so later than dace, and that could make life difficult for the little chaps' offspring.

Still, perhaps it's not that at all. Perhaps the dace are just sulking because people aren't throwing in as many maggots these days. Or maybe they've now got a taste for luncheon meat and we haven't offered them the right brand yet.

CHAPTER TWENTY SIX

Some people never learn

With some attention you, too, can be a better fisherman. But the question is whether it's worth the effort or not – and if you try too hard you'll change the name of the game.

A man said to me once "You've been recommended as one who can improve my casting."

Then he said would I very kindly come and drink his scotch one evening and help him put a fly all over his lawn. I said yes. Then went away and practised wildly in my own garden. Just so that I might be up to the job when I got to his. It didn't help that the person who had put my name forward as a kindly tutor of vast experience had been a guest I met just once at some dinner when talk was cheap and expertise not provable.

The exercise on the beginner's lawn started badly. That was because when he made his first cast I could see that he wasn't a beginner. In fact he was better than me. At least on grass he was. But I'd drunk his scotch and he seemed so darn keen that I could scarcely give a modest grin and tell him I was really a beachcasting expert and there'd been some mistake.

You know, it's not all that difficult, posing as an expert. Your pupil is so anxious to keep on casting that you only have to do it once or twice yourself. Then you stand back and pick up small points.

Being a very small expert but an awfully big theorist, I was able to explain interesting historical differences between casting styles. You know, the elbow-strapped-to-body style, the elbow-rising style with aiming thumb brought up to the eye, and so on. We didn't get to the double-haul because he wasn't a reservoir man and, anyway, what I know about that technique is not worth even a sniff off the top of a scotch bottle.

In a session interrupted only by the soft swish of Bentleys and Jaguars on the gravel behind the peacocks, I'd been a bit liberal and progressive about rigid twelve-noon rod tips – allowing a bit of drift back as the line extended behind his head. Then I corrected his pause on the backcast, tidied up his left-hand pull and gave him a refined comradely clap just to instil confidence and end on a high note. Fortunately, he was concentrating so hard that he didn't notice I'd meant to give him three claps, but he only got two. My hands missed each other on the third try. He had produced good liquor.

He didn't actually ask me to come again, which is just as well, since I don't think I could have stood the strain. Funny thing though, my own casting improved slightly after that.

With bottom fishing, things are rather more difficult, and that's probably due to the fact that so much more takes place under the surface of things. The plus point for those taken for experts is that you can't do quite so much in the back garden. Well, you can study to throw dollops of groundbait into a distant bucket . . . but that's what I meant when I said that you have to decide if it's worth it. No, for the coarse fisherman it's largely a self-improvement job, with a little help along the way when you meet a kindly mentor who may or may not know more than you, but probably does.

Of course, you must be prepared to listen when people tell you things, even if they know nothing about quick-sinking and slow-sinking monofil, say, or wire-stemmed trotters, or peacock quills with three inserts. And you do know all this and more . . . for all the good it does.

There was this gift of a swim. Fast run to the right downstream, slow run in the middle merging with a slack on the left. And me on a bit of bank jutting out into the middle of that lot of choices.

It happened that I'd decided what I wanted to do almost before I got there. If you are interested in degrees of nonsense then that is pretty nearly at the top of the list. Preconceived ideas, like heads full of theories, mean that decent anglers should stay in bed until it all wears off.

But I wanted to test a new big-wheel centrepin and needed some brisk current for the purpose; also I rather like brisk currents. So while I had a choice of swims from the same seat, I fished a small Avon trotting float down on the right.

A passing local said I should be fishing the slack on the left. He explained about the perch there, among other things. Though I filed away that message, I was bemused by the way the centrepin was operating and the hours just spun away from me.

With two small chub in the net and the day dwindling, I switched to the left-hand swim, quiver-tipping with fixed paternoster tackle and no more than a swanshot of lead. Honestly, it was a bite to every cast. Pull. Tug. Run. Twitch. Perch, perch. Chub. Roach. Perch, perch . . . I bowed respectfully in the direction of the village, accepted that I could have had a day to remember, and put it down to experience or arrogance, or both.

Some people never learn, though. Take this truth I'm telling from the present season, when I started hacking out this stuff instead of improving myself. Just the other day I was trying a new river and assessing things a bit before tackling-up.

My main trouble was having taken too many rods along to fit too many theories. But it must have seemed that I was staring into space because I was baffled by the water, for the man in the next swim up came quietly over and spoke words so discreetly that they appeared to be wrapped in a plain brown cover.

"Three rod-lengths out", he hissed. "No more", he added. "Needs a 24-inch trail hard on the bottom with a blockend. You'll be all right."

I thanked him and, when he was gone, tackled up with a 13-foot match rod, float and single maggot on a size 18. Some hours passed. I don't know about a painted float on a painted stream. Mine was deep-etched there for ever. Right, fall into the "change pattern" routine. Fiddle with the shot. Fish under the surface, at mid-water, and laying-on . . . trying all depths and measurements in between, English and metric.

Came a swirling sort of splash from the next swim up. And another. And a third. I went to look.

"All chub so far", he said.

"Well done", I said.

With humility, I returned to my swim and reached for the leger rod in the pile. It wasn't there. What I had was a stiff 8-foot spinning rod, packed by mistake. Another case of too much theory and too little common sense.

After a few minutes spent thinking about the value of legering with a 13-foot match rod instead, I set up the 8-footer and rearranged the rod-rests so as to operate more or less parallel to the bank. Then in with a blockfeeder filled with maggots and hook on 24-inch trail, as the wise one had told me at the start. I tightened up to the rod tip, which gave an immediate double-nod. I struck and missed. Refill feeder, rebait and cast out again . . . Nod . . . Missed. Theoretically speaking, the reason was probably rod-resistance, from fish who did not intend to be caught on anything other than a quiver tip or, at the very least, a weapon designed for the job.

So I arranged for more slack line under water and the next bite was a flickering kind of nod which gave me a nice dace. Right, I thought, we're away. We weren't. A lot of time passed, during which I heard more wallowing noises from the next swim up; and even, I thought, the creak of a landing-net handle being asked to handle too much. But managing it.

The light was dying towards packing-up time, when the rod tip gave a small bounce followed by a long lean forward. I thought it was weed and sort of lifted the little rod half-heartedly, turning it into a ghost of a strike towards the end of the lift. Then I knew there was a good fish on.

He leant on me and wouldn't show himself. The rod followed his movements in a stiff little arch. I eased him up, and he grudgingly broke surface a little. It was a roach. A special roach. I could see coarse scales and red fins. I could see his thick shoulders and expression of doleful surprise. I could also see the moment when the hook came out.

For a second he lay there, suspended between my failure and his success. Then he was gone. Don't tell me about 2 lb roach. This was 2 lb plus. Very plus. So just don't say anything at all. I'm going away to improve, all by myself.

CHAPTER TWENTY SEVEN

Evening class

On the home river Grannom were up in great sprays. You could almost feel the effect of massed tiny wingbeats. There was an occasional swirl – perhaps one or two in an hour seen while moving up from the bridge to the weir and back again. Pretty much the way of things on our water. The trout are there, but they don't like to put on a show.

That was a morning when April moved into May and everyone had cast his clout ten days before because there hadn't been an April like it for heat in 35 years. Three chub were being unusually delicate under trees, nosing sub-surface and keeping on station. Which is what the trout should have been doing, and weren't. Or if they were, they were being very secretive about it.

After using the upstream nymph, it was switched for downstream work, leaded a little against the push of the current. No response. Then it was something drably Grannom-ish on the surface, though fishing dry on this stretch of the middle river is never an optimistic operation.

Then it was something tatty and wet, across and down. Also to no purpose. Those sedges had been filling the air for some days so perhaps the fish, having fed hard, were now fed up. Or perhaps – and this is more likely – I was doing something wrong. Or a lot of things wrong.

There are days like that when you are reduced to flashing a Butcher around. It's an easy fall from grace when the trout are unco-operative and the rules of the water are pretty flexible. Next and final stage is a small spinner, better still a fly spoon; but the word is out from the Secretariat that they rather hope we won't do that.

Sometimes this scattering of life over the river in a particularly pleasant spring, this sense that something must show itself in a takeable manner, leads to despair. No, not despair, because that kind of emotion is out of place on a nice day. Rather, it's the feeling that something should happen at the next cast, but you know it won't.

In other places, where signs outside gravel pits advertise trout fishing in the same way as a garage offers second-hand cars for sale, people are inclined to get angry with the condition of nothing happening. Of course, there are some put-and-take fisheries which put in fish for puritans or allow them to be taken only by anxious ascetic types with barbless hooks. As it happens, these can be pleasant places, carefully managed and well spoken of in one or two of the few remaining good angling magazines . . . But even here people want to flash a Butcher from the first go, and keep on doing it. Except that they use something heftier and with a far more modern name. Once I saw a man trying to cast a concoction called a Dog Nobbler which sort of scrambles away. You can almost hear it barking as it goes.

Watching one or two (or thirty) fishers bashing away and trawling mighty lures through the clear water of one such Used Trout Lot, can lead you into holy smugness or utter disgust. Alternatively you can just ignore it. The other course is to join the crowd and do the same.

It is not so much the methods that worry you as the attitude they represent. Now documented as fishmonger angling, it is the greed in the voices that puts a nasty edge on things. They call to their friends: "Have you got your limit yet?" or "One more for my limit". And, worst of all, "I'm nowhere near my limit – when are they going to stock this place properly?"

The last time this went on around me I was mildly and righteously aiming at particular fish with a tiny brown nymph. And getting them. Just happened to be doing the right thing for that small water on the advice of the owner who likes to see his fish caught, but not nobbled. But would I have felt so . . . well, so decently traditional, if I had taken nothing and the lurid ones were spreading theirs out all over the well-mown grass?

If you feel the need to make excuses for hamfisted conduct then it takes no great brilliance of mind to do it. Plainly, we have created the demand and are satisfying it. You pays yer money . . . A man becomes a fox in the chicken-house or, rather, a rogue among the rainbows. After all, we have diminished the trout, taken him to the level of chickens. He is no longer a spotted fellow who comes as a surprise among the dace. He is ten a penny, though it's far more than a penny. And anyone can cast a bit of fur and feather doing his sums as he fishes.

When I was talking about reservoirs in an earlier chapter it was obvious that you can find the same attitude on small waters. Yet it seems worse in the more intimate places. Mind you, nobody thinks too much about it, because fishing does mean trying to catch fish. Only poets or poseurs would take a rod to an entirely barren lake in order merely to be part of nature. The fish must be there, or you are Simple Simon fishing in a pail.

Let me say, though, that even those who care shouldn't assume that the slaughter-urge cannot touch them. In places where you walk in the steps of fine and thoughtful men, there comes a moment when too many fish are showing all at once. Then the killer instinct flares up.

This is the famous evening rise on the chalk stream. The river fat with promise, the goods displayed in thunderous fashion. Never mind gentle sipping rises; solid and energetic trout take to the sky like dolphins on display.

At such periods we know that even the best man can lose his reason, and fumble and cast too many times before moving off to do the same thing again to fish after fish. And you leave after sunset, with aching wrists but only the fading excitement to show for it.

There was an evening in July when great splashes continued right through the half-light madness and made nonsense of such a distinguished stream. The noise of the fish was matched entirely by the swishing of rods.

Five rods were out on this long section and I was the only one not swishing. The reason was that my first and only take had been met with a strike of such savagery that I deserved the loss of the fly and the fish.

That, of course, is another aspect of the evening rise in earnest. When a fish does spot your artificial among all the live ones (or when you cast properly with a fly of the right shape and size, which sits up nicely for a change) you are so surprised that you act like a blundering fool.

By then I had come to a chastening conclusion, anyway. You just can't be sure what a fish is feeding on. Indeed, he may not know himself. It might *seem* like that steady fall of exhausted egg-layers, but it's probably something of invisible size instead. So your carefully presented Sherry Spinner just goes on spinning uselessly.

I wound in the remaining line, having resigned out of self-disgust which, of course, is absolute defeat. Water-licked, as some say. Or, as an old friend liked to remark in certain balmy days well remembered: "You have not troubled the scorer."

Well, there we are, then. I moved away from the bank for the quiet walk back while the splashings and rollings and leapings still went on. I nearly stumbled over a mound, or a small bush. It moved slightly and said "Nice evening".

He was sitting in a thinker's position, staring at the water. His rod was over his knee. Since I'd been flogging in that area for half an hour and no-one had walked into view, then obviously he had been there for half an hour at least . . . without fishing.

I moved away a bit as the pigeons began their final calling before lights out, and then stopped to watch as the thinker rose to his feet and got some line out. He did it with ghostlike gentleness in the gloom. Without sound. Economically, persuasively, effectively. His rod arched over the light from the river and a good trout came to the net. Then he moved up a few paces and, almost as if by pointing a finger at his selection, had another.

This was a good fish, which took him some time. Yet when it was on the bank and in the bag, it still seemed hardly to have broken the easy rhythm of his advance. Then the man lit a cigarette, clipped his net back on his belt, reversed his rod and went off into shadows on his way home.

You wouldn't think of asking him what fly he'd used because, while it might have mattered quite a lot, it didn't seem to be an important part of the lesson. He had come and gone as an owl might, making no mark upon the scene but still taking from it through deadly peformance once action was decided upon.

It seemed to me that he had not sought, greedily, to grab at pleasure just because there was so much on offer. He had not flung and floundered and lathered the water with sweaty demands. He had watched and waited, decided, acted, achieved and was satisfied with his brace. This was the classic approach to trouting. Or, shall we say, the classic image of trouting.

Nonsense, you say. He was just a competent bloke working out the shortest way to his brace. Maybe.

CHAPTER TWENTY EIGHT

Stop it right now!

If all your years are measured by rod, pole or perch, that's still no yardstick. You can't mark fishing days by blazing achievements, though never forgotten are the difficult fish, the surprising fish, the enormous fish or the hole you discovered in your keepnet at weighing-in hour.

You can cling on to the matter by remembering the natures of rivers though, their problems and their pernickety ways. It's easy to see them as personalities. The happiest anglers – though not the best – are secret dreamers with dirty fingernails.

But whatever the dedicated angler may be like – pale watery romantic, calculating technician, natural wizard, dogged Mr Average (that's me), or foul-mouthed slob – he must know that he is a hopelessly drugged wanderer who can only benefit from addiction.

As I've said in this book, an absolute love of angling may not be all that good for you. When even blank days merely make you look forward to the next, which are bound to be better, you get to thinking that life's a kind of big Mars bar.

Certainly, fishing is a celebration of life and living. Still, since that is such a big matter to celebrate it passes in a blur of days because we note them by way of things that seem small . . . the way the float cocks and slides under, the way the fly falls or the rod tip twitches. While we look forward to the beginning of those days, we cannot bear to consider their ending. Not to fish any more! Imagine it.

In my younger days I saw a fine angler at work on every visit to the home river. Always in harmony with the way things went, well or badly. But always netting dace and roach. He was committed to the whole of the matter.

In later years, he was still there – but struggling. Arthritis had him by the hands. It twisted them up. We all watched that process with a deep dread which was unspoken and guilty, of course, but well-recognised. Dread for him, dread for ourselves, dread on behalf of all those whose grip slackens upon the rod which connects them with so much more than the sporting moment. At the end he was turning the reel-handle with his knuckles. Then we did not see him by the river again. Indeed, I never saw him again at all, anywhere.

Well, worse things happen. But tell me of a real angler who has got to the heart of it and yet would hang up his rods tomorrow without feeling at least a hint of a kind of death? Tell me that and I'll say he's a sensible sort; and maybe I've known two or three of the kind, who are wiser than most. But I won't really believe you.

They say that as you get older the world moves faster. Too true. Forget the proverbial teenage policemen. Recently I talked with a colonel involved in planning for a World War Three counterstrike across the north German plain and he looked young enough still to be working out the map sign for a church with a steeple.

Any moment now some bright person will come up with the answer to this illusion and we'll be able to slow things down. Living each moment is part of the formula, and taking no thought for the morrow fits in somewhere too. But there's a missing element and we must hope that this can be wrapped up in some kind of pill to be taken before the first cast and after the last.

I do think that anglers need special consideration here. For most people, time started acting quickly like this when they became middle-aged. For us, it started when we had our first fishing rod.

On the river recently I decided that I'd have a good go at grabbing back the hours, since I could see that eight or nine of them weren't going to be enough. It was a perfect float swim, with things beginning to occur on all sorts of levels. The big dace were cropping up one rod-length out, after their smaller companions had been sent to investigate and found it good there. But I was missing too many bites.

In the middle swim in front of me lurked a few chub, deep down and wanting more than a single maggot. On the opposite bank, where the main thrust of the river was sorting itself out into a smooth glide, I was sure I had a line of grayling and had already netted a couple. I was working towards getting all the species together in the same place through a (for once) effective groundbaiting system. But suddenly I caught on to what was happening. The world had started turning awful fast.

So I stopped for a pipe which, naturally, broke the groundbaiting sequence without slowing time at all. And it was no good sighing and pretending it was boring catching all these fish, in the hope that this would cause the questionmaster to stop the clock out of sympathy.

That's how it goes, so often. You set out your tackle. You fish. You look up, and the day has gone. Morning and afternoon have been washed away in the current. All the hours have sunk in the eddies. The bee has quit the clover and your English summer's done.

Still, old Kipling also said that the trail was always new. Not that he was talking about catching dace, but he's right enough for us, at any rate. There's always tomorrow, or next Sunday.

I was trying to think of a day that I wanted to end quickly for a change. An awful day. A time-dragging day, when I said to myself that all anglers are mad. Well, there was that day when I sat under the green brolly in the longest, heaviest, coldest rainstorm ever known. It was a sub-standard green brolly and half the rainstorm was taking place on my neck. People who say that anglers enjoy rain should be given as little attention as you pay to those who say that anglers have to be patient. The first suggestion makes you sneer and the second makes you lose your temper.

All right, I don't mind a bit of rain as long as it stops for a moment at least. This rain did not stop. It allowed me to put the line through the rings and then just arrived in a rush.

When rain gets down your neck you curse but don't collapse. When it gets between wrist and shirt as you try to control the float, you grin and bear it. But when it is so heavy that it blots out all visibility and dictates your fishing method for the rest of the day (legering) . . . well, then you think about packing up early. Going out on the lead should be a careful and precise activity – it is made hopeless by constant discomfort. There have been a few days like that, and others when extreme heat made me wonder if the lake might disappear in a cloud of steam during the next half-hour.

And there was yet another type of day I remember, when I fished in a biggish national competition on a smallish canal. Nothing wrong with the weather. Everything wrong with the water. Ugly and shallow. Fifty-five boats and a hundred towpath walkers to every fish, and that fish on a distant section.

But times like that only join the blur of days when you

choose to remember them, which is not very often. Perhaps if we could have days like that pretty regularly then the hours would go more slowly. But who wants to strike that sort of deal?

Beside proper fisheries – and I don't mean ditches filled with brown fluid, or holes landscaped by steel teeth and the needs of the building industry – you are carried along by your own history. It's as simple or as complicated as that.

The living river flows before you from the constant present to all times past. It is a demonstration of the movement of time for you alone, since you are part of it by choice and need. But even if you just see the river as a repository of fish and all the rest as a load of old chat, there is one piece of advice which I feel bound to offer. Be grateful.

For good or ill I have marked out my undistinguished days by the flow of the stream and too many have gone for me to think that this is anything to moan about. What if I hadn't known so many? Join me in a shudder for the deprivation that might have been.

I have fished in school uniform on school days. I have fished in khaki when I should have been sweating in another kind of school before the wrath of the riding master. I have fished on my honeymoon and in my sleep.

What's more, I intend to go on fishing to the last cast, the last thumping trump, the last poundsworth of gentles or the last fire we light in the sky. Or till the rivers all run backwards. And if they do that, then I can start at the beginning again.